Hospital Quality Assurance

Models for implementation and development

Christopher R. M. Wilson, Ph. D.

W.B. Saunders:

1 Goldthorne Avenue
Toronto, Ontario M8Z 5T9, Canada

1 St. Anne's Road
Eastbourne, East Sussex BN21 3UN, England

West Washington Square
Philadelphia, PA 19105, USA

Cedro 512, Col. Atlampa,
06540 Mexico, D.F., Mexico

9 Waltham St. Artarmon, NSW 2064

Ichibancho Central Building
22-1 Ichibancho, Chiyoda-ku, Tokyo 102, Japan

94 Granville Rd., Tsim Sha Tsui East
Kowloon, Hong Kong

Canadian Cataloguing in Publication Data

Wilson, Christopher R.M., 1934-
   Hospital-wide quality assurance

Bibliography.
Includes index.
ISBN 0-920513-04-2

1. Hospitals—Canada—Quality Control.   2. Health
facilities—Canada—Quality control.   3. Quality
assurance—Canada.   I. Title.

RA983.A1W55 1987   362.1'2'0971   C87-093196-2

Last digit is the print number: 9 8 7 6 5 4 3 2

For LOUIS,
who always has all her ducks in a row.

Contents

CHAPTER IX

Foreword

The progress achieved in the last few years in the field of Quality Assurance by Canadian health care institutions has been so impressive that we often forget that the need for a formalized program was suggested only a few years ago.

At a time when the Canadian Council on Hospital Accreditation saw fit to include in its standards the requirement for a Quality Assurance program, there were many who searched for a practical approach to its implementation. Even today, for many institutions and individuals, that search continues.

Christopher Wilson has been, since the beginning, an enthusiast and a pioneer in this field. Through collaboration and consultation with the CCHA and other organizations, he has recognized the need for a program that not only would satisfy the requirements, but that, most of all, would be of practical value to the people working in the health care field. In doing so he has developed an adult learning model, not in a theoretical manner, but by testing it in the field and in real situations.

This book is the result of multiple experiences and practical applications. It is not a guide to installing a Quality Assurance program as a package; instead, it shows how to interest and involve those persons who will ultimately have the responsibility for the program. Only then, I believe, will Quality Assurance become a live and meaningful activity.

The book is an important resource to health care institutions and to the Canadian health system. Its approach will enhance the professional lives of all those who work within it.

Fulvio Limongelli, M.D.

Acknowledgements

The material in this book was developed in the course of consulting for member hospitals of the Ontario Hospital Association (OHA) from January, 1985, through May, 1986. In fact, the last lin ᐧ of this book should contain the adage: "Necessity is the mother of invention," because all the models and methods featured in the text were developed or discovered in response to the needs of client hospitals. Thus, the first acknowledgement must address the health care facilities whose QA implementation I was asked to direct, and their QA Committees who worked and learned with me: Hogarth-Westmount Hospital (Thunder Bay), Five Counties Children's Centre (Peterborough), Queen Street Mental Health Centre (Toronto), Hôpital Général de Hawkesbury and District Hospital, St. Thomas Psychiatric Hospital, Central Hospital (Toronto), Deep River and District Hospital, Hôpital Général de l'Ouest Nipissing (Sturgeon Falls), Ross Memorial Hospital (Lindsay), Sault Ste. Marie and District Group Health Association, Rainy River Valley Health Care Facilities (Fort Frances), Riverdale Hospital (Toronto), and Dryden District General Hospital.

The very satisfying experience of learning together with groups and individuals began with my collaboration with James Miller, CEO, and the QA Committee at the Whitby General Hospital. They have good cause to feel a sense of parenthood to the *adult learning model* which we discovered together in the winter of 1985.

I have been particularly fortunate in my colleagues at OHA. They have provided a highly supportive environment in which to experiment with new concepts. If I were to list all those whose encouragement had been important to me, it would include 25 to 30 people at all levels in Willis Rudy's Member Services Division. Instead, they must let me record my appreciation of five colleagues or groups in particular: Ronnie Bacher and Audrey Nelson share of job of being my secretary and have worked splendidly with each other and with me, handling the clients, arranging my travel, looking after my bookings, billings, and publication deadlines. They have provided stability to my professional life and have both played a major part in the completion of the final text in the spring of 1986. Judith Blake has been my partner-in-crime since early 1985; in the course of directing many QA implementations, she has both tested the models contained here and with her colleagues developed the generic departmental manual, *Nutrition and Food Services Quality Assurance: Getting Started* (OHA, 1986). Joyce Park has edited practically everything I have written at OHA, including *Quality Assurance: Getting Started* (OHA, 1985), the success of which emboldened me to go the extra mile. While she has not edited this text, she has advised on every chapter in detail at some stage of its development. The OHA Media Services—Bev Ross, Director, Alicja Debowski and Kellie Katsabas, Artists—have been a pleasure to work with, in translating my hazy concepts into bold figures that get the point across. Stuart Roberts has been my boss for eight adventurous years at OHA. I do not think he has read a word of this text or looked at a figure, yet he has made them all possible, encouraging me to take the QA bull by the horns, expecting me to find practical means for hospitals, and supporting this and other writing endeavours.

I will follow the English practice of *not* commenting on the contributions or deprivations of my family related to this writing endeavour—though I am very conscious of both. Outside of the Association, however, I must record my appreciation of: Fulvio Limongelli, MD, FRCS(C), the former Executive Director of the Canadian Council on Hospital Accreditation, who rightly deserves the title of "father of Quality Assurance in Canada." I have enjoyed his friendship and many discussions of QA and its importance and processes; Gerry Mungham of W.B. Saunders of Canada Ltd., who believed in this project from the beginning and has been unfailingly supportive over the long period of its gestation; Stanley Colbert of the Colbert Agency who likes writers and has made a virtue of supporting and representing them; and three associates, Rosemary Hill, Joanne Watson, and Paul Allen, who read this manuscript in first draft in November, 1985, and gave me their support.

Formal acknowledgement and appreciation is tendered to the following individuals and agencies for permission to publish copyright material:

The Ontario Hospital Association for permission to reproduce the Figures and Exhibits, all of which are the property of the Association, except Exhibits 27 and 28, and quote from its publications: *Quality Assurance and the 1983 Standards* (OHA, 1984), *Health-care Housekeeper* (Jan. 1985), and *Quality Assurance: Getting Started* (OHA, 1985).

Aspen Publishers, Inc., publisher of M. Lamnin's *Quality Assurance in Hospital Pharmacy: Strategies and Techniques* (1983).

National Health and Welfare for permission to quote from its *Dietetic Department Guidelines in Smaller Health Care Facilities* (Ottawa, 1979).

The Canadian Council on Hospital Accreditation to quote liberally from its 1985 acute-care standards, *Standards for Accreditation of Canadian Health Care Facilities* (Ottawa, 1984) and reproduce Exhibit 28, which was taken from material distributed at the Surveyors' Conference April 8, 1986.

The Canadian Hospital Association for permission to reproduce an Exhibit from the September-October, 1985 issue of *Hospital Trustee* from the article by S. Stacey, M. Henderson, and F. Markel (9(5), pp. 24-5), carried in this text as Exhibit 27.

The AMA/ACHS Peer Review Resource Centre to reproduce Figure 15, which first appeared in print in the *Australian Clinical Review* 21 (6), June 1986, p. 64.

American Hospital Publishing, Inc., for permission to quote from J.E. Orlikoff, W.R. Fifer, and H.P. Greeley, *Malpractice Prevention and Liability Control for Hospitals*, 1981.

In addition, I wish to thank Lois J. Bittle of Bittle & Associates, Inc., and the Ontario Hospital Association, for permission to quote from her paper, "The Board's Responsibility in Quality Assurance," presented to the Ontario Hospital Association, May 16, 1986.

Exhibits

Figures

Abbreviations

A/D/T	Admission, Discharge and Transfer
AHA	American Hospital Association
ALM	adult learning model
CCHA	Canadian Council on Hospital Accreditation
the Council	Canadian Council on Hospital Accreditation
CEO	Chief Executive Officer
CHA	Canadian Hospital Association
CME	continuing medical education
COTA	Canadian Occupational Therapy Association
CPR	Cardio-Pulmonary Resuscitation
DON	Director of Nursing
Dx	diagnosis
HBEP	Hospital Board Effectiveness Program
HMRI	Hospital Medical Records Institute
HRA	Health Records Administrator
JCAH	Joint Commission on the Accreditation of Hospitals
the Joint commission	Joint Commission on the Accreditation of Hospitals
JCC	Joint Conference Committee
LPTP	Laboratory Proficiency Testing Program of the Ontario Medical Association
MAC	Medical Advisory Committee
MAT	Medical Audit and Tissue Committee
MD	Doctor of Medicine
MHEI	Maryland Hospital Educational Institute
1977 Guide	*Guide to Hospital Accreditation,* 1977 (Ottawa: CCHA, 1977)
OH&S	Occupational Health and Safety
OHA	Ontario Hospital Association

OMA	Ontario Medical Association
OR	Operating Room
OT	Occupational Therapy/-ist
PAC	Professional Advisory Committee
PRN	as circumstances may require (Latin: *pro re nata*). Usually of medications or treatments
PT	Physiotherapy/-therapist
QA	Quality Assurance
QC	Quality Control
RM	Risk Management
RN	Registered Nurse
RNA	Registered Nursing Assistant
RT	Registered Technologist
S&C	standards and criteria
SHAPE	Saskatchewan Health-Care Association Program of Education
the *Standards*	*Standards for the Accreditation of Canadian Health Care Facilities*, January 1985 (also "the *1983* Edition")
TB	tuberculosis
UR	utilization review

CHAPTER I

The Nature and Purpose of Quality Assurance (QA)

1. QA as Confusion

Quality assurance—what does that mean?

Everything to do with an organization, all of the pieces of its structure that control and channel its life: the hospital mission statement, its organizational chart, its reporting relationships and job descriptions. Set at three of its four corners will be its policy and procedure manuals—administrative, patient care, personnel, and at the fourth, whatever passes for an overall theory or model of management—if there is one. Quality assurance is performance appraisal and measurement, standards and criteria, nursing audit, norms and peer review. Once we get all of these things together, they will fit together and the edifice will be the real Quality Assurance we have been looking for.

Quality assurance is advice. But it may mean confusion when helpful and knowledgeable people say different things and do not deal helpfully with other people's concepts. Quality assurance always means questions. The only answers available are expensive, or they don't fit, or they demand you start from another premise.

Quality assurance is paper. It has weight and mass, and is very heavy. It is also anxiety: the job is too big, time is short, and all the crossroads have six turnings. They are all marked "short cut" or "right way" and "long way," leading to "true way" and "safe way."

Quality assurance is anger. People are angry because the maps are wrong, and the guides unreliable. Practitioners are angry because they have patients and full-time jobs that are important, and they want something more, something new. They think: No, it won't help me take care of my patient; it won't give more time, more staff, more money. It won't make the job easier to do, and if it is going to help one poor fellow, I'd sure like to find him . . . Thank goodness, there's the telephone. Someone real, someone asking for me, something I can *do*, instead of going round and round in circles. I will go and do it and forget about QA. But I am angry and frustrated. Next time I won't wander round, I will start somewhere and do something—even if it means eating dinner's dessert before breakfast.

Some day someone is going to come along and say, "This is what QA really looks like" and I'll say, "By gosh, it does. But at least we got a piece of it right." I hope to heavens he says, "Well, so you did," even if he smiles as he says it.

2. QA as a Promise of Performance

I grew up in England in the 1940s and 1950s. My life was dominated by large institutions, schools, colleges, hospitals, the military, and I trusted them and the fairness of their administration. I also trusted members of the professions—doctors, lawyers, teachers, bankers, government officials, and so on. We *all* did. I dare say people of the same generation in Canada were also brought up to trust the inherent benevolence of the institutions in the public and private sectors that governed the fortune of society.

But no more. We can no longer trust banks when banks fail, or hospitals where dreadful accidents occur, or the police when they use violent interrogation methods, or schools where teachers strike. The list goes on and on. Every institution and profession has a black sheep in its family, whose misdeeds have provided alarming or sordid breakfast reading. Thus society, and we are society, says: "Before we give you our money, our trust, our bodies, our children, answer these questions: how do you know how good is the service you are offering? What evidence do you have that you can show us and which convinces you that your care, administration, service, teaching are what you say they are, and are what we want to receive?"

The answer that I give, as the provider of the service, is Quality Assurance. It is the *act of assuring, the evidence, guarantee or earnest of what I am promising,* and the *state of certainty* which should be shared by the provider and the client.

3. QA as Communication

Whatever else Quality Assurance may be, it is first and foremost a *message* from one person to another, attesting to the quality of something they both believe to be important. We have confused this matter by using the term QA to refer also to the gathering of data that support our statement. But we must again and again return to the notion that QA is a message. It is communication.

This morning I had someone in my office who was seeking help with QA for his hospital. Much of the confusion expressed in the first two pages of this chapter was inspired by his account of what his hospital and its staff were feeling about Quality Assurance. Finally I went to the blackboard and wrote:

QA is measurement.
QA is communication.

He had no trouble with that, so I expanded on "communication" by drawing a line from the bottom of the board, which I labelled "General Staff," to the top, which I labelled "Top Management." I turned this into an arrow, with the explanation:

> Here is the communication, from the point of service, the general staff, through the organization to top management and the board. The message is the quality of care or service provided.

Still no problem. Now I had to put "measurement" and all the bits and pieces of QA that he had into the same sentence as communication.

> Let's think of QA as a railroad. You have stations—let's call this one Audit, and this one Standards, and a main line we'll call Mission, and a branch line: Job Descriptions. We can go on labelling sorting yards and repair depots with the names of such other institutional features as Organizational Charts and Reporting Systems, but until we put the first train with the first carriage or goods wagon on the rails, we haven't got a railroad. The whole system only comes to life and operates when things and people are carried on its lines.

The analogy with QA was obvious; all the structured elements were enhancements to a system of transportation. The moving train is QA. Only when the transportation/communication system is operating can it employ in a meaningful way all the structures that are available—stations and lines and yards— policies and procedures, performance appraisal and credentials.

4. QA as Good News

"Quality Assurance has been an unwritten component of health-care delivery in Canada for most of the 20th century," wrote a housekeeping manager in the OHA newsletter (*The Health-care Housekeeper*, January 1985, p. 9). The writer was saying, in effect, that QA is something everyone has been doing for years but not recording. When a hospital pays a management salary, it is expecting the recipient to take responsibility for the quality of his or her operation as well as the resources employed in it.

When I meet with department heads and head nurses to launch their QA program, I ask them:

"What are you doing by way of Quality Assurance?" Glum faces; no answer. So I try again:

"How do you know what sort of job your people are doing?"

One by one, the answers come forth: "By inspecting," "Talking to patients," "Checking the tapes," "I taste the food," and so on. When I want to move them from the immediate awareness of performance to a longer-term assessment, I will ask:

"How do you monitor your department's performance, how well it is doing?"

Again, there will be a set of answers including statistics, incidents, feedback from physicians and other departments, quality control procedures and, in some cases, assessments made by external authorities.

By this exchange of questions and answers, I wish to demonstrate to my audience two things: first, that QA is something they are already doing in a variety of legitimate or valid ways. Second, I need to show them that QA is the communication of a new sort of management information. Traditionally, administration has required management information from department heads in two kinds: statistics and explanations. Monthly statistical returns have commonly dealt with both dollars (actual versus budget) and workload measure (numbers of procedures, patient days, radiographs, etc.). Explanations are what administration wants *now* about what happened this morning, yesterday, last week; explanations relate to the incident report, or complaint, that just hit the CEO's desk. The request is to clear up this bad news, and do it now.

Quality Assurance does involve the investigation of incidents, but its primary orientation is the reporting of good news and not explanations for bad. Department heads in a QA program are expected to report on a regular basis how good is their operation, how they know, and how they are planning to improve its quality or reliability. In this sense, administration is looking for a new sort of management information. In another sense, it is not new information at all. The three questions I used above with the department heads are almost synonymous, but because they had not been accustomed to reporting quality, the question about quality assurance efforts provoked no response. I could gain access to their quality assurance activities only by referring to direct supervision (How do you know what sort of job your people are doing?) and overall management (How do you monitor your department's performance?).

The housekeeper we quoted at the beginning of this section could equally have written: QA has been the best-kept secret in hospital management in recent years. Hospital managers have been taking responsibility for quality for many years. But they have never told anyone, because no one has asked— except about bad news. Quality Assurance has all the time been a private preserve maintained daily by front line staff, and monitored by the supervisor or manager, expected by but never reported to anyone outside the department. CCHA's 1983 *Standards* have changed this forever. They demand that quality and its pursuit come out of the closet.

5. QA as the Achievement of Goals

Philip Crosby is completely uncompromising about quality. For others quality means excellence, the unattainable star, goodness or that indefinable character that can only be recognized when it is there. Recently the American Management Association published as its first-choice book for managers John Guaspari's *I Know It When I See It: A Modern Fable about Quality* (New

York, AMACOM, 1985). For Crosby, and many others who have drunk from his well, all the above is so much fluff. "Quality is conformance with requirements," says Crosby. Did the specifications require a tolerance of 1.2 cm? Is that what your widget measures? If so, that is quality. If not—why not? Even if the specifications were wrong or inaccurate, delivering the product in conformance with them is quality in the person or section that produced the goods. There is much else in Crosby that deserves to be read, and both his books (*Quality Is Free: The Art of Making Quality Certain* [New York: New American Library, 1979] and *Quality without Tears: The Art of Hassle-free Management* [New York: McGraw-Hill, 1984]) are recommended without reservation.

The Council's starting point in QA is related to Crosby's standard. CCHA defines Quality Assurance as first, "the establishment of . . . *goals*; second, the implementation of *procedures* to achieve those goals; third, the regular *assessment* of performance relative to the goals; fourth, the proposal of *solutions* to close the gap between performance and goals; and fifth, documentation and *reporting*." Functional goals are the focus of all QA activity and are mentioned specifically at each stage until the last when performance (relative to goals!) must be documented and reported. There is nothing fuzzy about QA. It is the discipline of continuously and consistently measuring behaviour against goals.

While this "discipline" may excite a negative response in the reader and the professional, goal-oriented behaviour has an important payoff. Articulated goals or standards allow people to discriminate between essential and needless routines, behaviour and documentation. They also provide the essential core, around which such management tools as job descriptions, procedure manuals, etc. need to be developed, kept up to date, and used.

6. QA as Participation

The topic of roles in Quality Assurance is reserved for the next chapter, but we can make two general statements that say a great deal about the character of the program. The *Standards* insist that QA is a hospital-wide program in which all organized departments and functions participate. There is no elitism and no dumping. Everyone, the physician, the therapist, the engineer and the volunteer should be involved in a program of accountability for the quality of his or her care or service. There is healthiness when all functions are treated alike in an organization whose outputs depend on everyone's cooperation.

The second interesting feature concerns the ownership of the program. Although QA is reportable all the way to the top of the hospital's organizational chart, to the board itself, the program belongs to the practitioner. The physician, nurse, RNA, cleaner, cook and clerk are the people in the front line, the people giving the care, creating the product, delivering the service. The program is theirs because it is the quality of their endeavours that is enhanced and reported in QA. Not only do they produce quality; they should be involved in determining its standards and engaged in its appraisal. QA is not a management exercise but a foot soldiers' campaign. Some programs will make the mistake of saying that the front line effects, while the supervisor measures and the manager sets, the goals. Goal setting may indeed be a management task, but the development of practical and appropriate standards and criteria must be a consultative process. Most important, the measurement of quality must be a shared responsibility. The alternative is an "us and them" situation, cops and robbers, in which the practitioners act out the old proverb: "What the eye does not see, the heart (of the supervisor) will not grieve after." The Achilles' heel of all QA programs is the join between practice and the appraisal of performance. If the same people participate in both aspects of QA, the report of performance and that actually delivered are likely to be closely related. When one is a staff and the other a management activity, we have cast off the lines and left the ship free to drift.

Keeping performance and appraisal together is not easy, in part because managers at all levels want to be able to report good news and not material that will embarrass them and their superiors. One way to soften the blow is to give departments an opportunity to develop and implement solutions to problems with their staff, before the latter are reported. But QA is intended to be neither a recital of perfection nor a hot-seat experience. Its goal is the identification and correction of systems faults and not the scenting of bad apples.

7. QA as Reward

Although many individuals have acknowledged or complained about the frustration, extra work and confusion they have experienced in the implementation of QA in their hospitals, QA is still perceived as a program of promise and one that can be made to work. In this final section, will look at some of the payoffs of a QA program.

7.1. Professionalism

QA enhances professionalism in two ways. At a collective level, QA holds the profession accountable. This means that physicians are not expected to police nursing standards or physiotherapy to set nutritional standards. So the decisions about standards, measurement and problem resolution belong with the clinical or service department. Of course if the department does not produce the goods, administration or the board will ask why. At an individual level, QA calls on each practitioner to act as a professional and practise his or her specialty—from housekeeping to neurosurgery—according to his or her best standards. Hospital and medical staff are asked to practise as if they had always an audience of peers critically appraising their judgement and skill. In calling on health care practitioners to uphold the highest standards and by providing opportunities for peer review and standards review and appraisal, QA provides the means and incitement to excellence in practice.

7.2. Regeneration

Hospitals are like ocean-going vessels; they take an inordinate amount of time to turn around. Ships have a momentum that carries them forward in their original direction for miles, in spite of their best efforts to respond to the call of "man overboard." People in hospitals feel the same about their institutions; important changes take years to accomplish. QA certainly will not make hospitals more supple or spontaneous, but it will make them more sensitive to problems and more responsive to the imperatives of practice.

In the bad old days, nursing, with its army of staff and large budget, did not have to listen to housekeeping. The laboratories could never question what they were receiving from physicians, and if the Out-patient Department did not like Medical Records' chart retrieval service, it was bad luck. These attitudes obstructed change. Not only could one department not influence the service it got from another, but its failure to do so caused it to question the usefulness of changing its own way of doing business.

Under the influence of QA, all departments are undergoing change. QA calls on them to provide the best service *and* to seek an appraisal of that service from their clients—patients as well as other hospital users. Because quality is no longer a private matter for each department, its reporting and improvement create new and powerful mandates for change. Those responsible for the management of the hospital-wide program will have to see that QA reporting is not subverted to a new means of organizational manipulation. If they can do that, hospitals should benefit immeasurably from the changes induced by consideration of quality of care and service.

7.3. Service

The expression "the bottom line" is a financial term. Considerations of how a decision will affect the final total had to be a major, if not the major factor in the decision. QA gives hospitals a new bottom line: the quality of care. It is not that quality of care has not always been important. It has. But we did not have a way of measuring or appraising it. The appraisal was individual: Dr. X says . . . the Director of Nursing advises . . ., or it was a judgement call: the MAC believes . . . In spite of all the difficulties of measurement in QA, Quality Assurance programs will generate data that give objective information about care and service levels. These will constitute a new "bottom line," and one which will be respected by board, medical staff and administration alike.

The ultimate promise of Quality Assurance is patient care that is more effective, reliable, sensitive and holistic. QA should give the patient and the community not only the promise of performance, which demand we recognized at the beginning of this chapter, but performance that fulfills the promises made.

8. Summary: Quality Assurance—1985

Since January, 1985, the author and his principal colleague at the OHA have been involved in helping hospitals organize their own QA programs. In the course of this work we have developed a simple implementation methodology called the Adult Learning Model, which is described in detail in Chapter III. Along with the model are individual strategies and a variety of hand-out materials, such as forms, terms of reference, and sample statements. Many of these materials will find a place in this text. "Quality Assurance, 1985" (Exhibit 1) is one of these hand-out pieces which we distribute to department heads when launching the program. We encourage them to use it in explaining QA to their staff. It is included here, as it provides a useful summary of the nature and purpose of Quality Assurance.

EXHIBIT 1

Quality Assurance, 1985

Quality Assurance is a management system by means of which we assure ourselves and others of the quality of work for which we have responsibility.

Quality Assurance is for everyone who works in a hospital, from the staff person who does the job and assures himself or herself that it is well done, to the Chairman of the Board who reviews the evidence of the hospital's attainments and assures the people of the community that they will be in safe hands in their hospital.

For us as professional people, Quality Assurance is a way of constantly improving standards and our frequency of attaining them. But QA is chiefly for our patients, who need our expertise and caring, not sometimes but always. Care must be expert, reliable and sympathetic.

Quality Assurance is defined by the Canadian Council on Hospital Accreditation (CCHA), the national agency that accredits health care facilities of all descriptions across Canada, as a five-stage process comprising:

1. The establishment of functional *goals*.
2. The implementation of *procedures* to achieve those goals.
3. The regular *assessment* of performance relative to the goals.
4. The proposal of *solutions* to close the gap between performance and goal.
5. The *documentation* and *reporting* of this assessment activity.

The Council insists that Quality Assurance should be hospital-wide, in that all staff and departments have a program of accountability for their care and service. Similarly, CCHA wishes to see that accountability for quality be rendered finally to the hospital's Board of Governors, the majority of whom are lay trustees.

For hospital-wide QA to work, the institution must encourage two related processes—the continuous *assessment* of quality in all departments and programs and the *communication* of problems and attainments through the management structure of the hospital. The hospital's QA Plan describes how both functions are carried out and assigns responsibilities for the program to individuals and groups within the hospital.

CHAPTER II

Organization and Roles in Hospital-wide QA

1. The Cast

In this chapter, we move from the what and why of QA to the how and the who, from nature and purpose to organization and roles. In Chapter I we sought the definition of Quality Assurance from the 1985 *Standards* of the Canadian Council on Hospital Accreditation (CCHA). We will use the same source in the discussion of organization and roles.

In the Quality Assurance section, Standard II: Organization and Administration, the Council lists five agencies within the institution that have roles in the hospital-wide QA program. These are:

- *The board*, which is to initiate and support the development of the program and determine its organizational structure and receive its reports;
- *Administration*, which is responsible for the organization and management of the total program;
- *A committee* (group or individual) through which the development and coordination of the program may be accomplished;
- *Medical staff*, whose existing professional QA activities must be encouraged and integrated in the overall program; and
- Other *departments and services* that are to develop appropriate mechanisms to evaluate the degree of attainment of their unit goals.

This section does not make mention of the *general staff* whose task is to deliver quality service and participate in its assessment and improvement. They must be listed as our sixth quality assurance agent.

Under Standard III: Direction and Staffing, the *Standards* give the facility the options of appointing a QA Coordinator or assigning QA roles within the existing organizational structure. We will need to return to the position of QA Coordinator, but at this stage can assume that his or her role will fall within the same area as the mandate of the committee listed by CCHA.

Further roles are assigned to the governing body, in Standard IV: Reporting, in that the board is the ultimate recipient of findings of QA activities throughout the facility. In the 1983 *Standards*, the task of evaluating the effectiveness of the total program is also assigned to the board.

At the same time that the *Standards* assign these QA roles, they recognize the validity of present structure and practice. As noted, they explicitly call for the integration and encouragement of *existing* QA activities. While they seem to anticipate the appointment of a QA Coordinator, they explicitly allow for other delegation of responsibility. They call for hospital-wide QA reporting to the board "by a mechanism that does not conflict with normal executive reporting channels" (p. 47). I see in these remarks three very significant commentaries on QA: first, that QA is not a totally new creation but a new system that builds on existing foundations; second, that facilities should adopt structures that work for *them*; and third, in spite of its importance the QA program is subject to the normal rules of governance and management within the institution.

2. QA and the Medical Staff

2.1. Medical Independence and QA

In North America, most physicians are not on the salaried staff of the hospital. Instead, according to privileges granted to them by the board, they are authorized to use the facilities of the hospital in their own private practice. Under this arrangement, physicians do not report or owe account to the administrator of the hospital, but to the Medical Advisory Committee (MAC), which reports to the board through its Chairman, the Chief of Staff. When QA was introduced to U.S. hospitals through the standards of the Joint Commission on the Accreditation of Hospitals (JCAH), there was the expectation that medical staff QA and hospital QA would be integrated in one centrally administered program. However, attempts at integration caused much frustration, and practical rather than theoretical considerations have blessed the notion of separate but related programs. Canadian hospitals have taken seriously the U.S. experience.

Attempts to involve physicians in a single hospital-wide QA program have generally been unsuccessful for a variety of reasons. Physicians act as independent practitioners and expect to take individual responsibility for vital clinical decisions. They surrender some of their freedom in participating in an organized medical staff. It is the price they pay for hospital privileges. But acknowledging the authority of the MAC and the Chief of Staff is one thing. Physicians look askance at the suggestion that their practice should be open to question by hospital management and staff through the auspices of a QA program. By the same token, they will participate in medical committees and staff meetings, however unwillingly, but will seldom allow the claims of non-medical committees to intrude on the time they must devote to their practice. Then, there is the matter of confidentiality. Physicians have to review their own cases with their medical staff or speciality colleagues. They are unwilling to do this before a multidisciplinary staff, and particularly where, as in Ontario, the proceedings of such reviews can be subpoenaed by the courts.

Although independence, poor participation and confidentiality may not appear to be powerful enough considerations to keep medical staff QA separate from the hospital's program, they are important practical issues. We can add one more. When medical staff have been corralled into a super QA program, either or both of two things have happened. Sometimes, physicians have become involved in that program to the detriment of the continuing program of medical audit; at other times, they have taken over the process of the QA Committee. This has led to the inappropriate control of the programs of the clinical departments and sometimes the deterioration of those of the support services.

For some of these reasons or often just because medical affairs are organized separately from the management of the hospital, health care facilities in Ontario with few exceptions have opted for a separate QA program for their medical staff. Psychiatric hospitals and facilities that employ the services of medical consultants rather than an organized medical staff are the chief exceptions to the general hospitals' model, which is illustrated in Figure 1.

2.2. The Medical Advisory Committee

According to the Public Hospitals Act in Ontario, and the Medical Staff By-laws of most hospitals in the province, the MAC is, in effect, the Quality Assurance Committee of the medical staff. Its task is to consider, encourage and promote the quality of patient care provided by physicians in the hospital. Its chairman, the Chief of Staff, and the heads of medical departments, who are MAC members, are vested with authority by statute to act upon complaints of inappropriate medical attention. If quality of care is the *raison d'être* of the MAC, then it is clear that the medical staff already has in place the structure it needs for QA. If there is a task, it is to see that the MAC adopts procedures that will enhance its leadership in clinical appraisal and improvement.

Since the introduction of Global Budgeting in 1969 in Ontario, hospital administrators have been keen to get physicians to take more of a role in financial decisions. Rather than allow administration to make the resource decisions that affect clinical practice, CEOs have sought the participation of medical staff. Operating booking systems, bed allocation and closure, ranking capital equipment purchases related to patient care, and the utilization of beds and diagnostic resources, have all been referred to hospital MACs. QA is a timely reminder that the MAC, whatever its competence, is primarily a QA committee and not a financial, political, nor management committee.

FIGURE 1

Hospital-wide Quality Assurance: Organizational Chart for the Community General Hospital

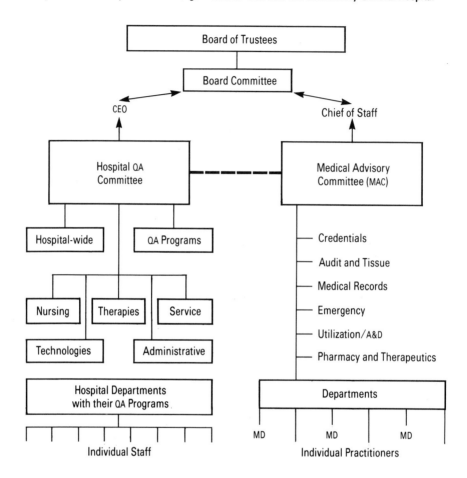

Two quite different structures report to the MAC: the organized departments (medicine, surgery, etc.) and the various MAC subcommittees, such as Admission and Discharge, Pharmacy and Therapeutics, etc. Under the impetus of QA, each chief or head should be expected to demonstrate to the MAC how his or her department is contributing to the improvement of quality and care and attention provided by the medical staff. The MAC subcommittees have surveillance over matters that cut across departments—Credentials, Medical Records, Emergency, Utilization. In contrast to the hospital monitoring provided by MAC, organized departments monitor practice on a vertical dimension—that is, according to specialties. We could draw this distinction in the form of a matrix, whose two dimensions, shown in Exhibit 2, serve the MAC well, allowing it to receive reports from both organized departments and subcommittees charged with the surveillance of common elements in hospital practice.

EXHIBIT 2

The Organization and Review of Medical Affairs
through Organized Departments of the Medical Staff and
Subcommittees of the Medical Advisory Committee (MAC)

MAC SUBCOMMITTEES	ORGANIZED DEPARTMENTS OF THE MEDICAL STAFF				
	MEDICINE	SURGERY	OBSTETRICS AND GYN	PAEDIATRICS	PSYCHIATRY
Admission and Discharge					
Audit and Tissue					
Chronic Care					
Credentials					
Emergency					
Infection Control					
Medical Records					
Pharmacy and Therapeutics					
Utilization					

2.3. Medical Audit

Although medical audit is nominally the responsibility of the Medical Audit and Tissue Committee, in fact the audits themselves are usually carried out in and by organized departments. Thus, they should be considered chiefly in the context of the vertical or hierarchical dimension of the medical matrix.

Medical Audit is a subject that should be pursued in its own right. It has been most competently addressed in the 1982 monograph *The Patient Care Appraisal Handbook* (Toronto: OHA, 1982), produced under the auspices of both the Ontario Medical Association (OMA) and the OHA.

In *Quality Assurance and the 1983 Standards* (with acknowledgements to Dr. Peter Tugwell and his colleagues at the Chedoke-McMaster Hospitals), I put the nine steps of the medical audit process in a "Clinical Audit Cycle," which is illustrated in Figure 2. When I look at the figure I remember two comments from Tugwell in conversation. I cavilled at the time it took to get the audit off the ground: four preparatory steps before the data were abstracted! He reminded me that the purpose of medical audit was behaviour change. At each of the preparatory steps, practitioners had fresh notice of what therapy was under review (Step 1), what criteria were important (Step 2), what the latest literature advised (Step 3) and by what standards they

FIGURE 2

The Clinical Audit Cycle: Medical Staff and Health Care Teams

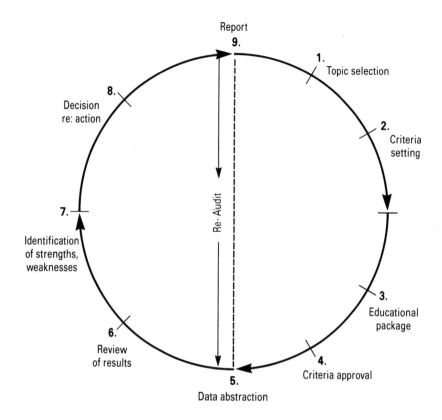

agreed to be judged (Step 4)—four invitations to change or improve. Looking at the left half of the cycle (Steps 6-8), Tugwell expounded on the need to "close the loop," to *act* effectively in the light of the audit's findings.

2.4. Medical QA in the Small Hospital

In Northern Ontario there are many accredited facilities of under 50 beds with a medical staff of half a dozen physicians or less. Their question to those of us who have put out a shingle marked "QA Expert" is, "How can we possibly assure quality?" The answer is that they can indeed operate a bare-bones QA program, based on the following practical suggestions.

2.4.1 Make a virtue of necessity.
According to the Public Hospitals Act in Ontario, an organized medical staff must have a Credentials Committee, a Medical Records Committee, and a Tissue and Audit Committee in addition to a MAC. With a small medical staff each of these committees will have essentially the same membership, but probably a different chairman. The suggestion is to have each committee focus on a review that can be part of the

medical staff's continuous assessment of its practice. The *year's* activities, including screening credentials of new applicants and up-dating the files of those already on staff, can be reviewed, summarized, and presented to the board/MAC as one audit. The quality of the medical record and the timeliness of its completion is always good for another. Death reviews, tissue reports, and OR complications are another good topic, as are the transactions of the Infection Control Committee, and so forth.

2.4.2 Explore the resources of HMRI. The Hospital Medical Records Institute (HMRI), which has computerized all the medical records abstracts from many provinces, has the power to analyze these data in dozens of different ways. In addition, the Institute has commissioned the development of canned audits on a variety of common disease topics. But all of this analytical power and its wealth of detail may convince the small hospital that HMRI is irrelevant to its needs. Many small hospitals cannot pull enough recent charts (25–30 in the past 12 months) to audit something as common as myocardial infarction. Here are two words of advice: first, there is considerable benefit in going through the prescribed process (per the *Patient Case Appraisal Handbook*) even in relation to ten charts. The learning involved in the review of criteria is of at least as much benefit as the review of the recent charts. Second, small hospitals should at least obtain from HMRI and review annually their profile of practice. This review, in comparison with previous years and the pattern of referral out, with judgements about both, would be a suitable topic for a QA report annually.

2.4.3 Pair with a similar facility in the same region. The problem in QA of the small hospital is the lack of data or experience with which to make good comparisons. One answer to this is to make an arrangement with a similar-sized facility in the same region, whereby both will carry out the same basic QA reviews and exchange their cumulative data. Such collaboration would be enhanced if a physician from the hospital pair were invited to attend the audit meeting and bring the pair's data.

2.4.4 Undertake interprofessional or team studies. There is always merit in looking at the care given to a patient or patients irrespective of the provider. Small hospitals that have difficulty in putting together single department studies (physio, dietetics, medical, etc.) are advised to undertake team or service studies. In these the questions are: "What services is *the hospital* providing to its chronic patients, and how effective are they?" or "How well did the hospital respond to trauma cases in the Emergency Department during the last quarter?"

2.4.5 Use visiting firemen. The final suggestion is that each major medical service offered by the hospital should be reviewed *annually* by an outside expert. These visiting firemen would (a) be chosen by the medical staff, (b) be invited by the hospital to come for the day to observe (including the review of charts), confer and advise the medical staff, (c) engage in some related Continuing Medical Education (CME), (d) be expected to dictate a one-page note to the hospital authorities on the quality of medical care in the specialty concerned (surgery, medicine, obstetrics, etc.) and (e) be paid a suitable honorarium by the hospital. I believe this to be an elegant and practical solution to the QA problems of many remote hospitals, which already have to depend on a host of outside experts to read their radiographs, accept their specimens, "supervise" their laboratories and, of course, accept their referrals.

This section has been somewhat longer than those that follow because we are now taking our leave of medical staff QA. Although physicians will be referred to throughout in the text, the book is primarily concerned with QA programs offered within the hospital, i.e. the non-physician hierarchy.

3. The Administrator as QA Architect

In my 1983 essay, I awarded only one sentence, in respect of QA, to the role of the Chief Executive Officer (CEO). The 1985 *Standards* are reticent about the CEO's role, whereas they have well in focus those of the board, professional staff, QA Committee/Coordinator and other hospital departments. In part, we are talking about the difficulty of defining management, for if management is the art of "getting things done through people," the manager acts only if and when others don't! In 1983, I wrote: "As well as being the architect and administrator of the hospital-wide program, the CEO is also its chief coordinator and the one who can ensure its comprehensiveness and the commitment of all staff" (Wilson, 1984 [ii], p. 25).

My experience of helping nearly 30 hospitals implement QA during 1985 and 1986 has impressed me with the number of important choices that have to be made early in the program, on very inadequate information. The role of the CEO in Year 1 of the QA program is to provide structure. His or her task is to make more right choices than wrong and keep things flexible enough to change directions when the path chosen becomes obstructed.

There are three key choices that have to be made in building a QA program.

3.1. The Logical Model vs. the Adult Learning Model

The most sophisticated choice an administrator has to make is what he or she wants the QA program to look like, and how it is to perform. Although it may come as a surprise to some, there is a choice. Many hospitals have opted for programs whose strength is in documentation, a careful construct of interlocking formulations (QA manuals, job descriptions, policy and procedure manuals, etc.). Based on this comprehensive foundation, there is a wide variety of audits designed to ensure that practice accords with these written standards. The other option is looser, more dynamic perhaps, but less secure. It calls for a minimum of new documentation and instead puts its investment in two features: the assessment of principal functions using multiple data sources and second, the communication of performance data up through the organization. I have tagged the two options the Logical Model and the Adult Learning Model (ALM). Each has its strengths and weaknesses. The orientation of the one is towards management and reliability, while the other stresses practitioners and improvements. Naturally, I cannot pretend to be impartial. I think there is a choice and that the choice really matters.

3.2. Involving Trustees

Between one-third and one-half of the hospitals I have assisted with their QA programs have wanted to involve their trustees in their *in-house* QA activities. There are two good reasons for keeping trustees out of the kitchen. Continuous QA is part of the day-to-day administration of the hospital. If trustees get involved at this level, how will they know when QA stops and management begins? I do not know any CEO who wishes to be second-guessed by a trustee on administrative matters. And even if the CEO and the trustee know the appropriate limits to the latter's involvement, will hospital staff who sit on the same committee? Why give everyone an opportunity for role confusion?

Yes, the *Standards* demand the involvement of the board, but in its normal role as the governing body of the hospital. If trustees are brought into the kitchen, they will become accustomed to the heat and sights and smells and be either unable or too willing to discriminate about the taste of the meal they have helped produce. The role of the board is to maintain its distance and appraise the findings of the hospital's and the medical staff's QA from the perspective of the layman—the patient or the family member.

3.3. Delegating the Management of QA

The *Standards* give the options of "a committee, group or individual" as the appropriate agency to develop and coordinate the program. There is in fact a fourth option: a coordinator serving with a committee. This latter is probably the most popular solution, certainly in Ontario. University Hospital, London has shown convincingly that a thoroughgoing QA program can be organized and operate *without* extra full- or part-time staff (a QA Coordinator). So there is a choice.

If it is the CEO's choice to employ a QA Coordinator, the *Standards* allow that the role "may be that of a resource person, stimulator or activator or it may be that of a data collector and correspondence secretary, depending on the role assigned to department or service heads within the organizational structure" (1985 *Standards*, p. 47).

According to the Council, the determining factor in the coordinator's role is the role assigned to department heads. In turn, their role depends on that retained by the administration and the CEO. Many hospitals have used their administrative council/senior management committee as the QA Committee, and have added the QA Coordinator as its agent to execute or supervise the carrying out of its policies. Usually this is a bad solution. Not only do senior management not know any more about QA than anyone else, but they are too far away from where it is practised to learn easily how it is done and how it works best. Meanwhile, they put the QA Coordinator in an unfortunate role as the most visible agent of a new imposition by management.

4. The Committee as QA Leader

Let me be prescriptive. Administrators should choose a committee to manage QA for them. The CEO will sit on the committee *ex officio* but appoint an assistant administrator (whatever the title) to the chair. The latter will report the hospital's QA program to the CEO, as a delegated responsibility. The committee should have at least as many department heads, who are responsible for their own programs, as it has other members. The Vice-president, Patient Services/Director of Nursing (DON) and the Health Record Administrator (HRA) should have seats, and, if possible, a physician should attend in a liaison capacity. All three of these people have useful connections with medical QA; the first (DON) and third (MD) may be members of the MAC. The HRA will be the principal resource person for the Medical Audit Committee. The hospital QA Committee may have other resource people, such as the Staff Education and Occupational Health and Safety officers. (See Exhibit 3.)

This structure has the merit of good delegation, good representation of those who are going to have to carry out the program, adequate liaison with medical staff QA, and some role security for the QA Coordinator, who will serve as a helping resource, and not as a compliance officer.

There are five leadership roles that have to be played by the QA Committee in the management of the hospital's program.

4.1. Program Management

Once the QA Committee has received the mandate to manage the QA program from the administrator, it must do just that. The Committee will set dates, recommend assignments, organize training, design forms, and secure participation.

4.2. Leadership

The QA Committee is not the armchair quarterback. Most of its members as department heads will be involved in modelling the behaviours they seek from their peers. In this sense, they are leaders and, to the extent that their programs work, coaches. The committee's primary role is to provide support and feedback to those developing QA programs at the department and section levels.

4.3. Reporting

The QA Committee has the difficult task of interpreting departments to senior administration and *vice versa*, as both are learning a new lexicon of quality

EXHIBIT 3

Composition of the Hospital's Quality Assurance Committee

	SMALL HOSPITAL	HOSPITAL 200 BEDS
1. Assistant Administrator: Nursing, or Delegate	1+	1
2. Assistant Administrator, other services		1
3. Head Nurse	1	1
4. Staff Development/Infection Control/ Employee Health Nurse	1*	1
Department Heads:		
5. Diagnostic Services	1	1
6. Service Departments	1	1
7. Treatment Services		1
8. Administrative Services		1
9. Health Records Administrator	1	1
10. QA Coordinator	__1__ 6	__1__ 10
11. Physician (liaison)	1	1
12. CEO *ex officio*	1	1

+ Usually Chairman
* Often as QA Coordinator

concepts. In later chapters, we will stress the extreme value of reporting. Feedback is equally important in preserving motivation and enhancing the sense of achievement that is possible with QA.

4.4. Evaluation

Although at the beginning of the program a QA Committee is unlikely to be discerning about the quality of the returns it receives from departments, it will learn quickly. And it will learn in the best way: by doing, by discriminating between substantial studies and quick studies, between masses of data and significant messages, between important inquiries and peripheral information. Fortunately, this discernment will grow as the departments' ability to undertake more significant and better studies also develops.

4.5. Monitoring the Interfaces

Although patient care is delivered by individuals, behind each of them stands a whole department, and behind that department stands many other departments, whose service supplies, facilitates or assists the department providing the direct care. The places where departments overlap or one service meets another we call the *interface* between the cooperating departments. When the coordination is good and the relationships cooperative, everything works well. Sometimes the charts are lost, the meals are cold, the specimens are late, the wrong patient brought or the supplies out of stock. The result, if you are fortunate, is improvisation and no real problem. If you are not, personal frustration and jeopardy to the service will occur. QA is not a solo performance, but a full symphony. It is comprehensive in scope. Ty Cobb, baseball's legendary hitter and fearless runner, used to say, "The base paths belong to the runner." In QA, we should say, "The interfaces belong to the Committee." If one department is prevented from meeting its own standards by the failure of another, it is the QA Committee's business. If a patient is embarrassed by the lack of coordination between departments, the QA Committee has a role. Whenever one department says to another, "That's not our job," the Committee should take an interest.

Figure 3 portrays the Committee's role as a series of tasks stemming from the initial mandate from the CEO. It directs the program through its many phases (2); it provides the leadership and resources (3); evaluates response to its demands (4); and provides feedback (5). When necessary, it steps in to correct intra- or interdepartment problems (6), and on a regular basis, even from the beginning, it reports the progress and results of the QA program to the CEO. Later it provides the text of the CEO's report to the Board.

The QA Committee is accorded limited space in this chapter, but it has the lead role in the next (III), which describes the initial implementation of the hospital-wide program. The Committee and QA Reporting, through which it manages the program, are the subject of Chapter VII.

5. Managers as Shareholders in the QA Program

The hospital has an operating budget, and each department or cost centre has its own budget which is a part of the whole. The hospital's budget may be monitored in the business office but it is controlled by the staffing and operating decisions of the cost centre managers. The QA program is analogous. It belongs to the hospital but its action, data, and effectiveness are all attributable to the various departments and their individual QA programs.

There are two reasons for the departments' independent ownership of their programs. Department heads are at once the senior echelon having distinct specialty or professional skills and functions, and the management level closest to those who provide care or service. If, as we established in Chapter I, first line staff *produce* quality, it is those who supervise them who *manage* quality, and the departmental programs that encourage and report their achievement. The hospital QA program is both a comprehensive and coordinated program; it is also a confederation of independent and free-standing programs. Both department management and the QA Committee will recognize and respect this duality.

In 1983 and 1984, it was easy to describe the essential shape of the

FIGURE 3

The Management Cycle: The Quality Assurance Committee

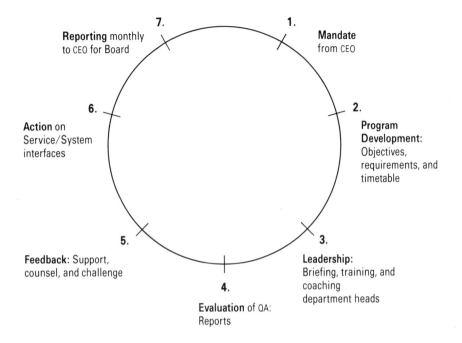

departmental program. It was the simple problem-solving loop: Identification, Assessment, Solution or Remedy, and Re-audit to ensure improvement. But the 1985 *Standards* have changed that. The new sequence described in Chapter I is: *goal* setting, goal-oriented *procedures*, *assessment* of performance relative to goals, *remedial action* if required, then *reporting*.

Instead of the simple Problem-solving Cycle that was used to illustrate departmental QA in 1984, the new cycle must incorporate both activities prescribed by the 1985 *Standards*: performance assessment and problem solving. Our Assessment-Audit Cycle is illustrated in Figure 4. In the figure the problem-solving or *audit* loop has been added within the *assessment* cycle which is the standard method of departmental QA.

The Cycle is labelled *assessment* and *audit*; these are the two essential QA measurement activities. By assessment, we mean the regular measurement of the quality with which principal functions are performed in the department. The intention of assessments is the comprehensive review of the department's primary work. Audits, on the other hand, are topic- or problem-centred studies, undertaken on specific occasions to investigate particular aspects of a service or system. The former should yield a report indicating

FIGURE 4

Assessment-Audit Cycle: Departmental Quality Assurance

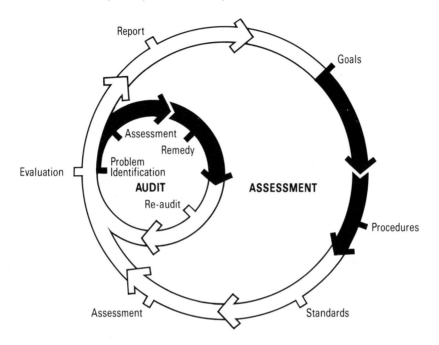

level of performance. The end product of the latter (the audit) is a solution or an improvement plan. *Both* activities should have a place in a department's QA program, like a net and a rod in the hands of a fisherman.

Later chapters (IV and VII) are addressed to department heads. Our task in this short section is to demonstrate the primary importance of departmental QA programs in the hospital-wide endeavour.

6. Trustees as the Guarantors of Care

The role of the trustee in Quality Assurance is described in detail in Chapter VIII, but there are four points to make in this chapter in which we review the organizational structure on which a hospital-wide program is based.

6.1. The Board of Trustees

The hospital's QA program and that of the medical staff inevitably meet in their independent presentations to the hospital's board of trustees. We have allowed for liaison between the programs through the administrative memberships on the MAC and MDs on the QA Committee (see Section 4, above). Whether these work or not, the first people who must hear both stories are the trustees. As such, it may be their role to bring the autonomous programs into closer cooperation.

FIGURE 5

The Community Cycle: Standing Committee of the Board of Trustees

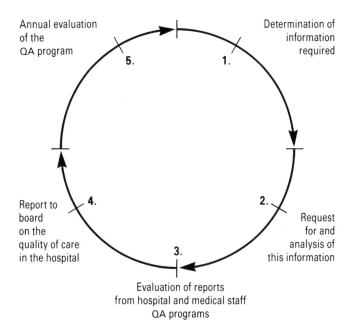

Annual evaluation of the QA program

5.

Determination of information required

1.

Report to board on the quality of care in the hospital

4.

2.

Request for and analysis of this information

3.

Evaluation of reports
from hospital and medical staff
QA programs

6.2. Determination of Information Required

Figure 5 shows the Community Cycle. Step 1 is labelled "Determination of information required." This is as good a time as any to make the point that all committees in QA have and should exercise control over what is submitted to them. I was visiting a CEO early one morning and found him in his office struggling with at least three inches of computer printout, and getting madder by the minute. Finally, he picked up the whole stack and with obvious relish threw it on the floor, with the words: "Damn Finance! Whenever I ask them for information they send me data." In QA all committees must say what information *they* wish to receive in what form, frequency, and detail. This admonition is particularly appropriate for trustees, who should insist on being addressed as laymen, as this is their essential role.

6.3. Other Information

As well as material which they see through the orderly process of the QA programs, trustees are also apprised of information that reaches them through other channels: the local newspaper, comments from neighbours, incidents, inquests and suits that are reportable by the CEO directly. QA programs and the process they use are ideal vehicles through which these negative data can be investigated and reported. The reports should say what happened in *this* instance, what generally happens (using data concerning contemporary instances), and what is intended to happen (the written procedure as the standard).

6.4. Trustees as Client Representatives

We referred to the trustees as laymen and women. They share this important status with patients, their families, and the members of the community. Serving in this capacity, they represent the clients in examining the Quality Assurance programs of the hospital. When convinced, the trustees give the community their assurance of the hospital's quality of care.

7. The Practitioner as Craftsman

The last cycle I described in my earlier essay (Wilson, 1984 (ii), pp. 21–3) was the Practice Cycle. Both the cycle (Figure 6) and the accompanying text are reproduced in their entirety below. I use the term practitioners to refer to the front line worker, the person who gives the care (physician, technologist, or orderly) or provides the service (pharmacist, cook, or clerk).

In undertaking a task, a practitioner is committing his or her training and experience to the achievement of a particular outcome in a specific set of circumstances. This is true whether one is baking a cake, teaching a patient, dressing a wound, doing a lab test or cleaning a room. Although practitioners seldom go through the process stepwise, they do *appraise* the situation, *plan* what they will do, attempt to *do it* and (this is where quality comes in) evaluate the results, *improve* on them if necessary, and then move on. Quality of care is an ingredient provided by the practitioner or not provided at all. The practice cycles of everyone who works in a hospital interlock to ensure quality; they are fundamental to any effective hospital-wide assurance program.

In Chartres Cathedral, the stone angels stand forever on their plinths 70 feet above the congregation, facing across the great aisle, their backs against the pillar they guard. Each one was hand-carved by a craftsman who devoted the same care to the statue's back and the inside of the wings as to those parts facing out. Only God and the stonemason have ever known the quality of the workmanship devoted to that unseen half of the statue. Some might say, "What an incredible waste of time and effort. If all those craftsmen had just attended to what had to be done, the Cathedral might have been completed as much as 40 years earlier." But this remark would have been just as unintelligible to the mediaeval cathedral builders as their patience and care with the hidden aspects of their work is to some of us. For them the audience was not man, it was God, to whose glory the cathedrals were built.

The health care professional in today's hospital shares two interesting aspects of his work with that of the mediaeval stonemason. The first is the hiddenness or secrecy in which his profession is practised; the second is the sovereignty of his own standards in defining the quality of his work. Let me illustrate with some everyday examples. Only the nurse changing

FIGURE 6

The Practice Cycle: Individual Hospital Staff

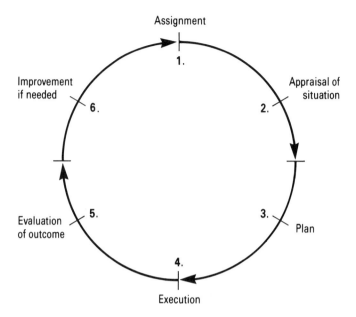

the sterile dressing will know whether she contaminated the field. Only the respiratory technologist will know how much better he could have handled the emphysema patient he treated at the end of the afternoon. Health professionals practise their art and skills in such privacy that traditional means of supervision and surveillance are mostly ineffective and would in fact be deterrents to care. Health professionals are crafts-men, and their fully rounded practice cycle, incorporating self-appraisal and improvement, is quite unlike that of the piece-work labourer who moves singlemindedly from the execution of one task to the beginning of the next. Although the hospital management has the say on what shall be provided to patients it is the craftsmen professionals who put their work into it.

The importance of a Quality Assurance program is that it encourages and rewards the quality they deliver.

8. Summary

This concludes our review of the cast of the Quality Assurance play. All members are essential in the general hospital system. However, there exist facilities in which there is neither an independent medical staff nor a board. These would include government hospitals, some treatment centres, nursing homes and others. Although we are writing about the implementation of QA in public general hospitals, QA does not end with them. By the end of this decade there will be very few human service agencies that will not be expected to show evidence of a functioning QA program. It is expected that their programs can be much simpler—as are their structures—than those of acute hospitals.

These are the essentials of a QA program:

- **Practitioners** give care and service with quality as they perform their roles in accordance with their highest standards;
- **Department heads** take responsibility for the management (quality and productivity) of the team they employ, and report on the performance of the department as measured against appropriate standards;
- **A committee** of department heads and administration reviews and evaluates QA reports, reporting their essentials to the CEO and advising department heads on its appraisal of their programs;
- On the other side of the house, the **Medical Advisory Committee** receives reports from the organized departments of the medical staff and from its subcommittees which monitor elements common to all medical departments;
- A committee of **the board**, or the board itself, receives reports from **the CEO** representing the hospital's QA program, and the **Chief of Staff,** representing the MAC. It calls for a review of other incidents or further information on matters that concern it, before giving its assurance to the community on the quality of the hospital's care and service.

CHAPTER III

Introducing Quality Assurance: An Adult Learning Model

1. Introduction

The *adult learning model* (ALM) for the introduction of QA was designed by the author in response to two significant dissatisfactions with the model used most frequently to introduce QA to hospitals in Ontario. It is undeniable that a mature QA program will depend heavily on quality assessments based on predetermined standards and criteria. However, the insistence on the development of a sophisticated and voluminous information base as a necessary first step in QA has been frustrating for many hospitals and, in some cases, a deterrent. The two dissatisfactions that are most frequently encountered with this model are duration and demotivation. New QA programs seem to take an inordinately long time to organize and make productive, seldom less than 18–24 months. And they often seem a drag. QA has a reputation for being a long, laborious, demanding, unfulfilling excursion into detailed documentation.

The adult learning model (Figure 7) began life as an attempt to assist a small hospital of about 100 beds to start its own QA program in fulfillment of Canadian hospital accreditation standards. The search was for a simple program that would work, i.e., provide regular information on the quality of the hospital's care and service, without the involvement of expensive resources (dedicated staff and/or computer) which the hospital could not

FIGURE 7

The Adult Learning Model for the Introduction of Hospital-wide QA

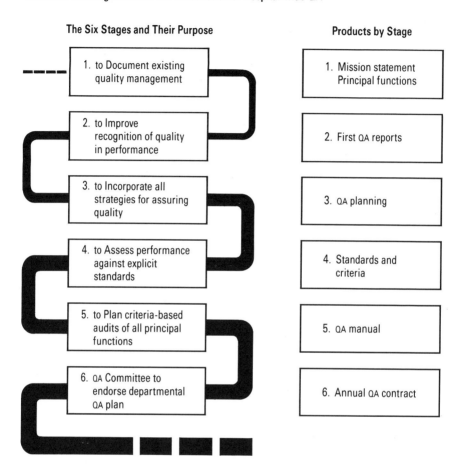

The Six Stages and Their Purpose

1. to Document existing quality management
2. to Improve recognition of quality in performance
3. to Incorporate all strategies for assuring quality
4. to Assess performance against explicit standards
5. to Plan criteria-based audits of all principal functions
6. QA Committee to endorse departmental QA plan

Products by Stage

1. Mission statement Principal functions
2. First QA reports
3. QA planning
4. Standards and criteria
5. QA manual
6. Annual QA contract

afford. It was reasoned that the more the program could utilize what was currently in place the more likely it would be to work. And there was the faith that if management could be shown the program at work, they would have the motivation and expertise to improve its scope and the quality of their information.

This concern to capture the systems in place meant that the department heads (including head nurses) became the principal resource of the program. Elementary QA had to be identified in what they were doing and new elements had to be introduced in such a way that they could be part of what was occurring. If the new demands were unrelated to the day-to-day management of the department they would probably not survive.

There was also the recognition that the program could ill afford failures. If one or two department heads became convinced that QA imposed impossible demands upon them, others too could find it inconvenient and unreasonable. To work, QA had to be (and be perceived to be) a user-friendly program.

Four discoveries occurred early that set the shape of the adult learning model:

1.1. Information on quality was found to be readily available to department heads, in that all of them in their own ways were monitoring the quality of their unit's operation. Thus if, with coaching, this information could be captured, it could also be reported. This elementary finding allowed the estimate of time required for QA start-up to shrink from a year or more, to three months.

1.2. The most effective means of teaching QA and introducing the changes in management that it requires was one-to-one coaching. By this means support and encouragement were given, and program demands that would otherwise have seemed harsh and unrealistic were negotiated and explained.

1.3. Success was "catching." Because the author/consultant did not know where else to start in coaching managers in QA, he began with those appointed to the QA Committee. When they found that they could manage QA in their own departments, the nature of the whole hospital-wide QA enterprise became transformed for them. It became manageable as a program and promised them personal and professional satisfaction. Committee members were on their way to being at least good ambassadors for QA inside the hospital. The more outgoing ones became coaches (Item 1.2 above) to their management peers.

1.4. QA is communication, the communication of information about quality of performance from the department to the governors of the hospital. Systems of audit and assessment are the means by which the department head arrives at better, more complete, perhaps more accurate, certainly more defensible, data. Standards and criteria are important tools in QA, not as masters of but as servants to the process. They help to transform soft and subjective data into reportable facts; they provide structure that leads to better assessment and monitoring.

In spite of their importance, however, standards and criteria (and other rigorous forms of documentation) belonged in our model to the later phases of program introduction. Reports from other hospitals underscored the extent to which prolonged attention to documentation in the early stages of QA had had a powerful demotivating effect. Thus our rule was: write standards and criteria/policies and procedures for *immediate* use. Managers will write them more willingly then, because they need them. They will write them best and most appropriately then, because they will have a forthcoming audit or assessment in mind.

EXHIBIT 4

Steps and Stages in the Introduction of QA (The Adult Learning Model)

2.1 **Structure:** Determine and put in place the organizational structure necessary to support a hospital-wide QA program.

2.2 **Launch:** Committee launches the QA program with an educational session for department heads and head nurses (managers).

Managers complete one- to two-page form giving their mission statement, principal functions and quality monitors in place (Stage I).

2.3 **Coaching and Feedback:** QA Committee members meet individually with managers to assist them to reach Stage I, and identify QA methods in place and immediately reportable. After the Committee's consideration of manager's responses, it gives written and personal feedback and support.

2.4 **Restructure:** Committee returns to the QA organization and makes provision, if necessary, for the activation of medical staff and trustees, through establishment and organization of a Board Committee.

2.5 **Monthly Reporting:** Committee develops report forms and storage and retrieval systems based upon the performance data received from departments. It begins reporting QA monthly to CEO for his/her transmission to the Board Committee.

Managers reach Stage II by virtue of having reported quality of performance to committee for three months (Stage II).

2.6 **Negotiation:** Committee calls on managers to develop a QA Plan for their unit/department/cost centre which indicates how and when they will assure *all* their principal functions.

Managers develop QA plan, to the satisfaction of their superior and the QA Committee (Stage III).

2.7 **Educational Support:** Committee proposes the introduction of Standards (S) and Criteria (C) to quality assessment and offers resources including S&C clinics for their development.

Managers introduce standards and criteria as basis for measurement of performance, for QA assessments currently being reported (Stage IV).

2.8 **Evaluation:** QA Committee reviews the department's standards and criteria and advises on their adequacy and improvement, and the appropriateness of proposed methods of assurance.

Managers develop S&C for all principal functions (Stage V).

2.9 **Contract:** Managers, their superiors and the QA Committee *agree on the content and frequency of the cost centres' QA reporting for the year (Stage VI).* These contracts become part of the hospital's QA Plan, subject to the board's acceptance and endorsement.

2.10 **Review:** Annually on the initiative of the QA Committee, the board reviews the implementation and adequacy of the hospital's QA Plan, and makes a report to the Annual Meeting of the Hospital Corporation on the quality of the hospital's care and services.

2. The Adult Learning Model

In the adult learning model, ten tasks (2.1–2.10) are set out for the managers of QA—the QA Committee, Coordinator or outside consultant—and six (Stages I-VI) for the department heads/head nurses (Exhibit 4). Often the tasks are related.

2.1. Structure

The essential first step for all facilities intending to introduce QA is determining who shall manage the program and how. The program needs to have the principal players in place, each with his or her part and authority from the CEO to play that part. The organization chart for QA should show the relationships between the players and should include the Board, the Medical Advisory Committee (MAC), the hospital's QA Committee, the department heads and the CEO, the Chief of Staff, and the QA Coordinator. The organization recommended for a hospital using our ALM is given in Chapter II, Section 2. It is of course subject to local preferences.

The determination of structure, which can be first a paper exercise, is just one part of this first step. Equally important is the *commissioning* of the QA Committee, which is seen as the all-important change agent in the introduction and development of QA. By commissioning we mean that the committee members must be so convinced of the viability of a QA program organized through the ALM that they are prepared to take responsibility for it as advocates and leaders. They also have to understand the process well enough to give reliable guidance as to the next steps and stages facing the department head.

2.2. Launch

The QA Committee's first responsibility is to organize a meeting of department heads and head nurses to launch the program. At this meeting QA will be explained to these hospital managers and they will be introduced to the first task they need to undertake in order to get the ball rolling. Their task, which they will work at with their colleagues, consists of the writing of a simple two-sentence mission statement, the identification of their principal functions, and an indication of the means they currently employ to monitor the quality of their department's care and service (Exhibit 5). Most managers will complete this task, albeit in rough, during the meeting and will obtain direct feedback on their responses from the facilitator and from their colleagues.

2.3. Coaching and Feedback

In the third step, the leader(s) will work with hospital managers one-to-one to refine the role statement, principal functions and quality monitors in place.

EXHIBIT 5

Foundations for Departmental QA

Please complete the following questions in planning your own departmental
Quality Assurance program:

1. Mission Statement

The role of the department is:
To

2. Principal Functions

*In the operation of the hospital the _____
Department is responsible for

●

●

●

●

●

●

*This sentence should be completed as often as necessary, listing in simple
statements the department's principal functions.

3. Quality Monitors in Place

The quality/reliability of the department's care/service is currently monitored by means of:

-
-
-
-
-
-

4. Other QA/QC measures that could readily be put in place are:

-
-
-
-
-

One-to-one coaching reinforces what was learned in the Launch, ensures that the manager's first submission to the QA Committee is in line with its needs and expectations, and confirms that the manager is competent to handle the demands of the QA program.

Because of the ALM's stress on early reporting, the leaders will be identifying all the means of assessment/quality monitors that are currently available for reporting to the Committee. This will almost immediately provide encouragement because it reveals how much information is already available.

As an example, on only the second day of the very first ALM program, the author was able to identify 20 current QA or Quality Control (QC) monitors from 11 different departments, in addition to hospital-wide programs with current quality data. Only three departments had nothing immediately available. Naturally, this revelation of material available to the Committee after just two days acted as a powerful confirmation of the soundness of the strategy the hospital had adopted.

Communication to hospital managers has to be handled in such a way that they receive both feedback and professional support. Sometimes QA Committees will assign to each of their members a liaison role with designated departments. This works well.

2.4. Restructure

Often it becomes clear to the QA Committee, as it gains control of its own responsibilities, that one or both of the other constituencies—the board and the medical staff—are as yet unorganized. The QA Committee does not have authority over, either, of course, but insofar as it may understand best the implications of hospital-wide QA, the Committee should raise its concerns with the CEO. It is then his/her task to get them to take responsibility for their parts in the total program.

2.5. Monthly Reporting

QA is sold to the hospital as a communications exercise. The program's principal task is to communicate, to the governors of the hospital and the community they represent, data on the quality of the hospital's care and service. The QA Committee has to gain mastery over the paperwork and learn how to communicate effectively in both directions—to the reporting departments and to the CEO for his report to the trustees. In reporting quality upwards a distinction should be made between communicating information about the *program*, and news from the assessment or audits of *performance*.

Although performance data are most desirable, both elements are important in intelligent reporting. In reporting the development of the program the committee will make reference to a series of stages through which departments pass en route to mature specialty QA programs (Exhibit 6).

A department is said to have reached *Stage 1* when it has an operating mission statement, has clarified its principal functions, and has documented

EXHIBIT 6

Stages in the Development of the Departmental QA Program

Stage I
The department has submitted, and revised to the QA Committee's satisfaction, a one- to two-page return giving the department's mission statement, principal functions, and QA/QC monitors that are in place or in preparation.

Stage II
Over a three-month period, the department has provided the QA Committee with data from single or multiple quality-assessment procedures.

Stage III
The department has met with the QA Committee and has developed, to the Committee's satisfaction, a QA Plan, under which it has proposed specific quality assurance procedures for all its principal functions.

Stage IV
The department has developed and tested (and had approved) standards, criteria and assessment procedures for the functions it is currently reporting (see Stage II).

Stage V
The department has developed, has tested (and had approved) standards, criteria, and assessment and other QA procedures for all its principal functions (as outlined in Stage III).

Stage VI
The department has established with the QA Committee a 12-month QA schedule indicating the frequency with which each function will be assessed and when the Committee expects to receive reports of the department's QA activities and results.

the methods of quality assessment it is currently using. After it has been reporting data from these assessments to the QA Committee for three months, we say that it has achieved *Stage II*. The QA reports from departments and from hospital-wide programs are grist for the QA Committee's mill. They are the substance of its reports to senior administration.

We can discuss the subsequent committee steps and departments' stages together as they are two sides of the same coin.

2.6. Negotiation: Departmental QA Plans and the Committee's Response

To this point in the program, all the Committee has been asking is that departments should do better than they were doing at Day 1. By better we mean more regularly, more conscientiously, and with better documentation. Now it is time for the Committee to ask for more activity. Its demand is that departments should return to their lists of principal functions, and develop a

QA Plan that will propose assessment measures for *all* those functions. The call is to broaden the scope of the department's QA program.

The role of the Committee is to make and explain the demand and then to support and act as a resource to department heads in their planning. All QA Plans should be endorsed in Stage VI and reviewed annually by the Committee.

2.7. The Introduction of Criteria-based Assessment: Demand and Educational Support

Having initiated departments in their QA planning, the Committee will introduce the demand for written standards and criteria. In *Stage IV* it will ask departments to introduce standards and criteria for the assessments they are already performing and reporting. And then in *Stage V*, it will ask for the development of standards and criteria for all the assessments promised in the department's QA Plan.

Delaying the demand for standards and criteria to this juncture of the implementation process (*Step 2.7* and *Stages IV and V*) is quite deliberate. The writing of standards and criteria has become a bugaboo, an inhibitor of the process, a major demotivator. Because of this we have chosen to show our clients that much assessment is possible with informal standards and that a functioning QA program is feasible in advance of rigorous documentation. We are also banking on the likelihood that well before this point in the program, department heads will have introduced standards and criteria to their assessments *on their own initiative*. This usually occurs when they feel the need for greater precision in what they are reviewing and reporting.

The stance of the Committee will be: (1) introduce standards and criteria when *you* need them, and (2) don't have your people write standards and criteria without actual audits or assessments in mind.

2.8. Evaluation

It may be only at this stage in the process that the QA Committee introduces criticism in its relationship with cooperating departments. To this point its role has been that of supporter, promoter and coach. In a mature program, however, the Committee must act as the evaluator of the methods of assessment and of the validity of the measurements used. It will act as a research or a new-products committee, testing the tools, methods and inferences, not to overthrow them but to enhance their credibility and usefulness.

2.9. Contracting for the Year

In the final step of implementation the QA Committee has to draw up a schedule that will indicate which departments report their QA programs and results, with what frequencies. Considered in the setting of the schedule are the frequency with which the CEO can report QA to the board committee, which does not always meet monthly, and the QA Committee's obligation to provide an appropriate response to departments reporting to it. The department's commitment to a reporting schedule for the year marks its achievement of *Stage VI*—a fully functioning departmental QA program.

The term "contract" is used because the program works best when the various parties indicate to the others what they will submit, what they will do with the data, and how they will respond to them. Nothing threatens the vitality of a QA program so much as the perception that reports are not being read and implications are going unrecognized.

2.10. Annual Review of Hospital-wide Program

Annually on the initiative of the QA Committee, the board committee reviews the implementation and adequacy of the hospital's Quality Assurance Plan. It should make a report to the Annual Meeting of the Hospital Corporation on the quality of the hospital's care and services.

3. Conclusion

The adult learning model is so called because it uses basic adult learning practices: coaching, learner support, beginning with present behaviour, and so forth (Exhibit 7). Originally, the author was prepared to grant that what

---

EXHIBIT 7

Essentials of the Adult Learning Model

1. Starts where people are.

2. Introduces the new as a modification of the old.

3. Introduces the the new as a series of single and reasonable demands that build to the total behaviour desired.

4. Involves a Steering Committee, which represents both
   - top level support, and
   - the level of management expected to get the job done.

5. Launches the program with an up-beat information session, which
   - establishes a timetable for whole implementation, and
   - concludes with the first demand and an early deadline (7–14 days) for its completion.

6. Keeps up the momentum with
   - individual feedback and support: coaching,
   - the next demands, and
   - regular reporting to the Steering Committee.

7. Schedules further information sessions
   - to demonstrate the handling of a difficult step, and
   - for feedback, including indications of success/program achievement.

---

could be achieved in three months would not be as good as what was being achieved elsewhere in two years, but now he believes that this assumption may be false. Misdirected efforts and time inappropriately spent have characterized the implementation efforts of many in QA. Canadian hospitals have all had to get on line at the same time with few, if any, good models before them. They have all had to do what we insist we should never need to do, namely re-invent the wheel.

The ALM works for two reasons: it is based on adult learning theory and has a strategic focus. We will deal with the focus first. In this model, QA is described as a communications program. Its goal is the communication of information on quality—which is already largely available where the care or services are delivered—to the lay governor of the hospital. Effort in this model then is directed at communicating data and not originating them. This distinction cannot help but save at least six months. It also has the merit that everyone is discovering QA together as they work in parallel.

The board, senior administration and the QA Committee are all gaining experience in handling quality data at the same time that department heads are moving from unsophisticated reporting to better measurement and a wider range of assessment.

Adult learning theory recognizes the significant differences between adults and young learners. Adults are impatient and action-oriented, they learn in order to do, and to do *now*. They bring to the learning situation a wealth of related experience and they learn by integrating the new into the knowledge and skills they have already. The ALM's insistence on starting with the management systems in place contrasts markedly with the logical demand that managers go back to the beginning and carry out extensive documentation before involving themselves in quality assessment.

In learning situations adults are vulnerable to their negative experiences of learning in the past and also to their fears of being shown up as incompetent in the new task they have been set. By insisting that QA is not new, the ALM shows people that they have in fact been carrying out QA in a dynamic fashion all along. ALM recognizes that adults, and especially working managers, are highly motivated to gain and maintain competency, and it relies on two established preferences in adult learning—adults learn most by doing the job, by practising the new skills; and adults typically learn through self-paced inquiry.

The adult learning model of introducing QA is essentially a strategy of growth, rather than an introduction of a brand-new system. It calls on different groups of hospital people—trustees, administrators, physicians, managers and staff—to transform their behaviours in the directions of quality enhancement and recognition and to take on different leadership roles in a re-orientation of hospital behaviour. Although the adult learning model was developed in the implementation of quality assurance programs, it is in fact a user-friendly strategy of wide application. In a recent article (Wilson, 1985) the author has described the model in generic terms and explored some of its possible applications outside of QA.

To the question, "How good will a QA program introduced through this model be?'' the answer is that the program will develop to the point where it matches the quality achieved by the hospital's other programs and services. In other words, you won't have an inadequate QA program—however it is introduced—in an excellent hospital, and *vice versa*. In the long run it is the quality of leadership that counts.

CHAPTER IV

The Four Essential Components of Quality Assurance

Speaking in June, 1985, in Toronto, Lois Bittle, a U.S. authority on QA, defined quality assurance as "those activities and programs intended to assure quality of care in a defined medical setting." Not a profound definition perhaps, but it appealed to me at the time because I had been struggling with the untidy mess of ways in which we assure quality. I was finding it difficult to relate ward rounds to criteria-based audits, yet realized that both activities had the objective of assuring quality. Bittle's definition allowed me to see that an activity does not have to be measurable to be QA.

In quality assurance there are four related activities: setting objectives, promoting quality, monitoring activity, and assessing performance (Exhibit 8). A QA program, when it is developed, should offer structured ways to provide for all these phases of quality assurance.

1. Setting Objectives

CCHA's definition of QA begins with "the establishment of goals," and goals must form the foundation of QA programs at all levels: departmental, medical staff, and hospital-wide. A friend used to remind me, "If you don't know where you want to go, any road will lead you there." So true. Goals and objectives state where we choose to go, and standards define important elements in the manner of our travel. Crossing the finishing line first is the goal, but the first runner across will not be declared the winner unless he or she has the baton in hand, and the other team members have kept the rules

EXHIBIT 8

Essential Components of Departmental QA Programs

1. **Setting Objectives**	Performance Standards	Prospective
	Management Goals	Prospective
2. **Quality Promotion**	Quality Investment (QI)	Prospective
3. **Activity Monitoring**	Quality Control (QC)	Concurrent
	Quality Supervision (QS)	Concurrent
4. **Performance Assessment**	Quality Review (QR)	Retrospective
	Quality Evaluation (QE) or Audit	Retrospective
	Quality Approval (Q3A)	Retrospective

EXHIBIT 9

Definitions of Performance: A Hierarchy

LEVEL	FORMULATION
1. Corporation	Hospital mission statement
2. Division	Goals and objectives
3. Department	Role (or mission) statement
4. Unit	Principal functions
5. Function	Standards of practice (and product standards)
6. Procedure	Measurable criteria

(standards) of the relay race. In the Hierarchy of Definitions of Performance (Exhibit 9) we could substitute "principal goals" for "principal functions" at Level 4.

The setting of goals and standards may be essential to QA, but it is not specific to quality assurance. It is a function integral to good management. This fact forbids our saying that QA begins with the setting of standards; it does not, simply because some standards have been in place long before QA came on the scene. Under the influence of the QA program, standards will be reviewed and revised. That is as it should be. The point to be made here is that QA programs can start with a full deck of standards and goals, if their agents know where to look.

1.1. Standards Prescribed by Others

We can divide goals and standards into two groups, according to their immediate origin. Some are developed *in-house*; others are established by *external agencies*. We will begin with the latter. External agencies prescribe standards for hospital practice at corporate, departmental and even functional levels. At the corporate level hospital affairs are governed by legislation, most of it provincial, because health falls in the provincial rather than the federal domain. In Ontario, the Public Hospitals Act and its Regulations are all important. But hospitals also come under legislation governing employment (the Employment Standards Act and occupational health and safety legislation) and as a business entity (the Corporations Act). Then there is a wide assortment of regulations and codes governing public health matters, fire preparedness, and building standards. Some governmental standards are enforced by inspection—such programs as public health, radiation safety, laboratory licencing, and in Ontario, the Laboratory Proficiency Testing Program (a government program delegated to the Ontario Medical Association). The intention here is not to depress the reader by lengthening the list, but to point to the immense fund of prescriptive standards that are available and appropriate to quality assurance.

The only standards I can think of that match and in fact exceed the comprehensiveness of the Public Hospitals Act are those of the Canadian Council on Hospital Accreditation. Legislation generally governs matters of administration and the environment, whereas clinical matters are addressed by professional bodies, some voluntary (professional associations) and others regulatory (professional colleges). The CCHA Standards are unique in that they concern administration and the environment as well as their primary focus, standards of clinical practice. Under the heading of clinical standards would be listed those of the Colleges of Physicians and Surgeons (of Ontario, and the Royal College), of Nurses and Pharmacy, and the long list of associations (including my own, the Ontario Hospital Association), but more properly those of the professions (medicine, nursing, pharmacy, physiotherapy) and the technologies (laboratory, radiology, respiratory and engineering).

It is worth referring to two other external sources, both of which are commercial. Insurance companies may set standards and even carry out inspections to see that standards are being met. Manufacturers also set standards for the safe operation of equipment and utilization of environmental and therapeutic supplies. These standards should also be part of quality assurance.

1.2. Setting Standards In-house

Then there are those standards proposed and promulgated by management. Exhibit 10 lists these as "adoptive standards" (in distinction from those that are "mandatory" or "prescriptive"). Under this heading would be performance goals, including annual budgets as well as standards for individual functions. Nine times out of ten, new standards need not be written for practical or QA reasons; instead, those responsible need to find and adopt, or take and adapt, a standard that has been developed already within or outside the hospital or department. Although not essential in a standard, there is some security in knowing that it has been developed and promoted by a body more authoritative than the immediate user. However, the latter has the

EXHIBIT 10

Common Sources of Performance Standards

Mandatory Standards (External Agency)
* 1.1 Health and hospital legislation.
1.2 Corporation and employer legislation.
1.3 Standards set by regulatory agencies, often enforced by inspection.
2. Regulations of professional colleges established under the Health Disciplines Act (in Ontario).

Prescriptive Standards (External Agency)
* 3.1 Manufacturers' advice.
3.2 Insurance company advice.
4.1 Standards of the Canadian Council on Hospital Accreditation.
4.2 Standards promoted by professional associations and teaching facilities.

Adoptive Standards (In-house Authority)
* 5.1 Hospital mission statement.
5.2 Facility's long-term plan.
5.3 Management by Objectives (MBO) statements.
5.4 Annual budgets.
5.5 Administrative and Personnel policy and procedure manuals.
5.6 Union collective agreements.
5.7 Job descriptions.
6. Procedure manuals in clinical and technical departments.

* Items 1, 3 and 5 are sources of *administrative* standards. Those numbered 2, 4 and 6 are major sources of clinical standards.

responsibility of testing the applicability of the standard before employing it or endorsing it for the department.

1.3. The Distinction between Standards and Goals

It is useful to make a distinction between goals and standards. A goal is a future objective, which may be general and not well defined. Hospital mission statements are full of goals. Goals set directions. They may not be stated clearly enough to distinguish those who have achieved them from those who have not. Budgets, similarly, are predictive statements, but not accurate measures of quality. If a department lives within its budget we do not know whether this was good management, good prediction, or low volume. Management by Objectives (MBO) statements, though more exact than mission statements, tend to show a range of achievement rather than a clear statement of attainment.

In contrast, a standard is a definition of attainment that can be described in the present. Administrative, personnel and clinical policy and procedure manuals define present policies and the means of attaining their objective. Procedures are written in a logical sequence of steps, and inherent in each should be one or more standards whose achievement can be verified.

Procedure manuals should be current and in evidence in all technical departments. Job descriptions and union contracts may be two further sources of employment standards.

I am indebted to Dr. Limongelli, the former Executive Director of CCHA, for pointing out to me that standards are enforced by Quality Control, which is a concurrent system designed to prevent undesired change (see Section 3 below). Meanwhile, goals and objectives, which are oriented to the future, are an integral part of what he called Quality Improvement. Performance Assessment (Section 4 below), like employee performance appraisals, consists of reviews of the past in order to make improvements in the future. Limongelli sees QA to oversee both Quality Control and Quality Improvement, the maintenance of standards and the achievement of goals.

2. Promoting Quality: Quality Investment

The quality of a person's performance is related to his or her own standards of performance—and skill in attaining them—and to the support system which rewards that performance. If either the personal or the support element is lacking, then quality of performance will be low or in jeopardy. If I am working for you, and to your standards, then when you are not looking I will work to my own standards—which may fall short of yours. If, on the other hand, I begin with high standards but my employer never indicates pleasure with the quality of my work, and lets others get by with less, how long will I bother?

Quality of performance is promoted by what I call *investment* activities. Performance standards have to be taught and the necessary skills developed, if new levels are to be achieved and maintained. When an employer builds training and development opportunities into the operating plan of the company, he or she is making an investment in the skills of the employees. Under the heading of *quality investment*, we can list:

- Staff training and development.
- Continuing professional education, through courses, institutes and conferences.
- The development of position descriptions leading to optimal recruitment.
- Employee performance appraisal.
- Employee suggestion programs—but these must be active, rewarded and promoted.
- Quality assessment procedures—these represent an effective investment in quality and its improvement.

But quality investment does not have to influence people only.

- New product evaluation, and
- Preventative maintenance programs

are also significant investments in quality.

As indicated, quality promotion will be prospective. The promotional activities can be recorded and reported but they do not entail measurement.

This lack of measurement distinguishes them from our third component: activity monitoring.

3. Activity Monitoring

Performance is monitored concurrently by two means: quality control (QC), and quality supervision or the surveillance by management. The two activities are distinguishable, in that QC is a continuous or routine *system*, whereas in quality supervision, the actions can be routine or occasional, but are *initiated* by someone in authority.

3.1. Quality Control

When the term quality control is mentioned, most hospital people think immediately of the laboratories and their heavy load of QC activities. Some will also think of radiology and dose measurement activities carried on to limit the amount of radiation given to the patient. Both are appropriate examples of QC, but they only begin to tell the story. Exhibit 11 lists those QC systems that would be found in place in most hospitals. Two additional systems deserve special comment.

EXHIBIT 11

Quality Control (QC) Systems

1. Finance	Daily and weekly balancing. Double signatures.
2. Nursing	Annual check of nursing credentials. Incident reporting, OR checklists, sponge counts, foot-printing newborns.
3a. Engineering	Weekly testing of back-up generator. Testing of all electrical equipment brought into hospital.
3b. Fire and Disasters	Monthly fire drills, evacuation procedures, extinguisher inspections.
4. Radiology	Film review prior to departure of patient. Temperature checks of processor. Dose measurement procedures.
5. Laboratories	Use of test samples. Daily calibration tests of auto analyzers.
6. Medical Records	Quantitative and qualitative analysis.
7. Pharmacy	Narcotic counts, ward stock inspections.
8. Rehabilitation	Infection control procedures with physio equipment and media.
9. Central Supply	Sterilizer tests.
10. Central Stores	Random inventory checks.
11. Food Services	Inspection of fresh food and vegetables on the loading dock. Hand washing and other sanitation procedures. Temperature checks of refrigerators and hot food.
12. Personnel	Performance Appraisal program.

3.1.1 Occurrence Screening.
This is still more common in the U.S. than it is in Canada. It is a concurrent review of the chart by experienced QA personnel. It is their task to spot deviations from procedures that could show a breakdown in protocol and, if allowed to go unchecked, may be the occasion of an incident or an adverse patient occurrence. What some Canadian hospitals do have in place is a range of events that are reportable or investigable. Many of these are in the medical realm, such as:

- Return to Emergency Room for same condition within 48 hours of first treatment;
- Single unit blood transfusions;
- Adverse drug reaction/interaction.

All of these events raise questions. They may not be "incidents," which we discuss below, but they demand review.

3.1.2 Nursing Audit.
Because of its concurrent aspects, this could be listed as a QC measure. This may call forth protests from nurses and thus requires explanation here. Nursing audits are undoubtedly audits, that is, inquiries about practice that are based on pre-determined standards and criteria. However, when we ask the question: What is the focus and intent of the concurrent elements? We have to answer (1) the evaluation of present care and (2) the immediate remediation of discrepancies discovered, and only (3) the aggregation of audit data to show trends and common problems. This focus on present care and its improvement consigns it, in our definition, to Quality Control—a concurrent system of performance monitoring and remediation. Thus (concurrent) Nursing Audit belongs in both categories: Activity Monitoring, and Performance Assessment (Item 4 below).

3.2. Quality Supervision

Inspection and incident handling are two forms of concurrent activity or performance monitoring carried out by someone in authority. The more important of the two categories is *inspection*, in which we include all those occasions when the supervisor, department head, head nurse, or charge technologist observes subordinates at work or the immediate results of their attention or inattention. Although in the examples that follow we have used negative data, negative events will always represent a small minority of the supervisor's observations, unless standards have broken down completely. Dirty hallways (housekeeping), patient in distress in a waiting area (radiology or emergency, etc.), poorly explained procedure (physio, respiratory, etc.), incomplete or messy trays leaving the belt-line (nutrition) would all be examples perceived by the supervisor, who would call for their immediate correction. The value of supervision in quality assurance is that it encourages and maintains high standards of performance. The recognition of good performance and the good performers, and recognition that poor performance is being noted and treated as unacceptable, are powerful elements in supporting superior quality of care and service.

The investigation of *incidents* is the second category of quality supervision. Although strictly speaking this is a retrospective activity, in that the incident *has* happened, the purposes of the investigation are (1) stop-loss and remediation of the present situation, and (2) correction of present practice so that an early recurrence does not happen. At a later stage, there will be an analysis of all incidents that have occurred over a three- or six-month period, but this is an assessment exercise, as described in the next section.

4. Performance Assessment

Performance is evaluated in three ways: quality review, quality evaluation, and quality approval. Before discussing each in turn, we ought to establish the distinctions between them. Quality approval is the term given to describe all those ways in which people *outside* the department assess or pass judgement upon the quality of the department's program or service. The other two means of assessment are forms of self-appraisal in which those responsible for the care form their own judgements as to its quality. Quality evaluation most people would term "audit," as the judgement is always based on pre-determined standards and criteria. Quality reviews tend to be less structured or formal. In contrast to the concurrent components of activity monitoring, the three forms of quality assessment are retrospective in focus.

QA professionals may be provoked at the length of time it has taken us to get around to the evaluation of performance through the process of audit. The delay has been deliberate. Of course, the retrospective and rigorous evaluation of actual performance against pre-determined standards is an important activity, but it is only one of eight QA activities described in this chapter and one of three assessment processes. It is done less frequently than almost all the other activities, and even when done is no more influential than most of them in assuring quality. This comment is intended as a statement of perspective and not as a snub to those who have a higher commitment to audit.

4.1. Quality Review

By quality review we mean to include those analyses of performance data that are done often on a repetitive basis to yield indications of quality of care or service. When medication and patient incidents, employee accidents or employee separations are reviewed for the previous quarter, the analyzers are making comparisons with the past and making judgements as to whether performance is better or worse. But chiefly they are looking for underlying trends that will guide them to appropriate action or the investigation of particular problems. Sometimes quality reviews are carried out with reference to pre-determined standards. Just as frequently, judgements are made on the basis of either the incidents themselves or in comparison with the performance of previous periods or professional or institutional peer groups. The central difference between quality reviews and activity monitors is one of timing: in the case of the former, the reviewer is looking at retrospective data to report a conclusion, whereas the latter monitor current data with a view to correcting or improving performance today.

4.2. Quality Evaluation

Quality evaluation, for many people, is the crux of QA, the criteria-based measurement of performance based on objective data. Medical and multidisciplinary audits, outcome studies, and structured program evaluations would all be primary examples of this key category of QA activity. As the next chapter is entirely devoted to the measurement of quality, little more need be said at this stage.

4.3. Quality Approval

All the strategies of measurement described to this point (quality control, quality supervision, quality review, and quality evaluation) have been strategies of self-assessment. With quality approval we incorporate the views of others. They come from three sources: external agencies, clients, and cooperating departments.

4.3.1 External Agencies.   Exhibit 10 listed both mandatory and prescriptive standards that were set for different aspects of the hospital's operation, and noted that some standards were enforceable or measurable by inspection. Here we acknowledge that these inspections/reviews are carried out, and recommend that the agencies' findings be treated as valid and significant performance assessment data. Of course, agencies work in different ways. Some come when they choose (the Ontario Ministry of Labour, the Public Health Department), some come after giving notice (Ministry of Health), and some do not come but request the facility's data and reports (LPTP and the Hospital Medical Records Institute). Some agencies come only on request or in response to a client relationship (CCHA; the hospital's insurance carrier).

The reports of external agencies should be taken seriously by QA Committees and Administration for three reasons. First, the hospital board has a right to be more impressed with the evaluation of an experienced outside body than with the hospital's self-appraisal efforts. Second, whatever bias the hospital may impute to the external appraisers, they are likely to be experts in appraisal—because they have appraised the same departments or functions in hundreds of other facilities, and repetition promises some objectivity and validity. Lastly, economy: every function that is to be appraised by an external agency is one less that the department need appraise itself.

4.3.2 Clients.   Hospital patients and their families comment on the care and service they receive in two ways: on their initiative—with bricks or bouquets; and on the hospital's initiative—in response to questionnaires or structured

interviews. These data require different treatment. Patient complaints (and commendations) should be treated as are patient incidents: investigated and reported as soon as possible.

Hospitals should use patient questionnaires sparingly. They tend to yield little usable information because they are poorly constructed and ask patients questions that they are not able to answer reliably. Organizers of educational programs use the term "happiness ratings" to characterize the essential message of program evaluations, submitted by students or by participants. So many patient questionnaires provide only a happiness rating. But they *can* be well done, even if they do demand special skills and experience.

Cooperating departments are also my department's clients, and it is quite valid to ask them to evaluate the service I give them. Consider the following example: a small hospital in Northern Ontario had its consulting radiologists evaluate the quality of the films it sent them to read. The radiologists cooperated in drawing up a quarterly evaluation sheet. The idea was good and is working well.

5. The Scope and Language of QA

The foregoing account is intended to provide two new dimensions to our discussion of quality assurance. First, it enlarges the scope of QA considerably beyond the usual boundaries. QA is not just standards and criteria and measurement and perhaps quality control. Quality assurance is not an arc but the full circle. We have taken Bittle's definition to mean *all* "those activities and programs intended to assure quality of care." Thus we see other elements in the CCHA's definition of standards, such as Staff Education, belonging within a QA program, rather than distinct from it. For us quality assurance is the unifying factor for a whole plethora of checks, activities, and routines that are part of hospital life.

Second, this chapter has provided a taxonomy or classification of quality assurance activities. As a student of QA, I wanted to know how it was done. The answer I received was peer review and audit and quality control—except that was not really QA—and some informal and not very reliable means, such as questionnaires. But when I went out to hospitals I found them doing all sorts of things and calling them QA. Sometimes I was asked to bless their efforts and tell them that they were in truth QA. But I needed a box with compartments, and I needed to know how a Public Health Department's inspection of the therapy pool was different from a medical audit, yet both were varieties of QA. Hence this chapter. The taxonomy or classification consists of Standards/Goals Setting and the six subelements Quality— investment, control, supervision, etc. This is the writer's third version of a classification; over the past year it has stood up well to the wide variety of QA activities that hospitals now employ. Readers are invited to use it to analyze their own efforts. One hopes it will provide a common language in which to discuss other institutional models.

Before leaving the four essential components (setting objectives, quality promotion, activity monitoring, and performance assessment) we need to add one note on the relationship between them. At first I saw them to have a linear and sequential relationship, thus:

1. ⟶ 2. ⟶ 3. ⟶ 4.
Setting   Quality   Activity   Performance
Objectives   Promotion   Monitoring   Assessment

After all, this makes sense. QA begins with standards (1); the standards have to be inculcated or taught (2); their attainment has to be monitored (3) in the present; and retrospectively, the entire product has to be evaluated (4) However, I noted an interactive relationship between standards and the other three components in that while each was dependent on the standards and goals established, their experience could force a revision of the same standards. This insight left me with
Promotion ⟶ Monitoring ⟶ Assessment in the same linear relationship as before, but with each interacting with Goals and Standards, set on a line above them. However, it was not long before I recognized that the data from Assessment is likely to change the content of Quality Promotion. This put all elements in interaction with each other, as shown in Figure 8.

FIGURE 8

Four Processes Complement and Correct Each Other to Achieve Quality Assurance

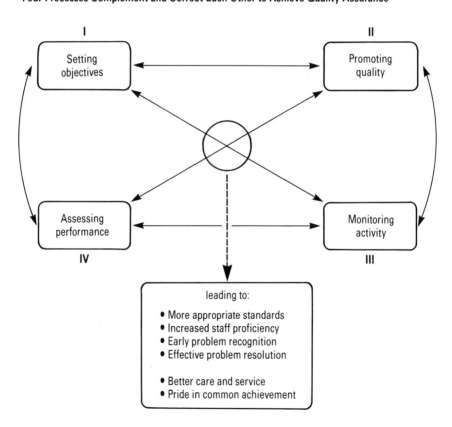

EXHIBIT 12

Some Examples of QA Components

	Examples	Subcomponent	Component
PROSPECTIVE	Annual goals, MBO statement Performance targets	GOALS	1. SETTING OBJECTIVES
PROSPECTIVE	Structure, process or outcome standards Rules/regulations; inspection standards Government or professional regulations	STANDARDS	1. SETTING OBJECTIVES
PROSPECTIVE	Staff development Individual coaching Performance appraisal Preventative maintenance New-product evaluation Safety drills Continuing professional/medical education	Q INVESTMENT	2. QUALITY PROMOTION
CONCURRENT	Concurrent nursing audit Temperature checks (Nutrition) Infection control Occurrence screening	Q CONTROL	3. ACTIVITY MONITORING
CONCURRENT	Management inspections Head nurse's rounds Investigation of patient/staff incidents Chart location review	Q SUPERVISION	3. ACTIVITY MONITORING

RETROSPECTIVE	Analysis of: Incidents
	    Film rejects
	    Sickness/absence returns
	    Mechanical breakdowns
	Specific nursing audits
	Observation of tray returns
		Q REVIEW	4. PERFORMANCE ASSESSMENT

RETROSPECTIVE	Medical audits Multidisciplinary audit Outcome studies Tray audits Program evaluation	Q EVALUATION	4. PERFORMANCE ASSESSMENT
RETROSPECTIVE	Hospital accreditation LPTP Radiation inspection Annual financial audit Supplier inspections OH&S inspection In-house service reviews Infection control Patient/family questionnaires and comments	Q APPROVAL	4. PERFORMANCE ASSESSMENT

CHAPTER V

Developing Departmental QA Programs

This chapter is written for and addressed to department heads, head nurses, cost centre or program managers—those, in other words, who are accountable to senior management for the quality of care or service provided by first line hospital staff.

1. Getting Started: Listing Principal Functions

However your hospital decides to get into Quality Assurance, whether by public statements, an education/information session, or a management memo calling on you to develop QA materials, sooner or later there will come that moment when you face the extent of the Quality Assurance demand and say "Where on earth do I start; what do I do first?"

OHA's Adult Learning Model is quite clear, as is CCHA in its definition of Quality Assurance. The first says: write down your principal functions and list the ways in which you are *currently* monitoring your department's performance. CCHA uses different words but the meaning is essentially the same. The Council's definition of QA begins: "Quality Assurance is the establishment of hospital-wide goals, the assessment of the procedures in place to see if they achieve these goals . . ." (*Standards*, 1985, p. 45).

So, whether or not your hospital supports the model of implementation recommended in this book, here is your starting point: you need to set out your principal functions/departmental goals on the one hand, and, on the other, list the assessments you have to monitor the achievement of those goals.

A principal function is an end product (or service) that your department is responsible for delivering. Patient meals, lab tests, patient care, health teaching, and equipment repair, are all end products of particular departments and could be listed as a principal function. The determination of principal functions/end products is the essential first step in QA planning, and the department's list is the foundation of its QA program. Without a list of principal functions you cannot decide whether a particular function is significant enough to require formal quality assessment, nor know how adequate is the scope of your quality assurance program.

We expect managers to develop in rough a workable list of principal functions in 15 minutes during our QA Launch, so the task is not difficult. Principal functions can be expressed in point form ("diet counselling," "sterilizing of instruments," "environmental control") or in longer phrases ("the vocational assessment of patients injured on the job" or "planning of educational programs for the whole hospital," and so forth).

The list of principal functions should account for 80 percent or 90 percent of the department's outcome, and should describe its products or services in a way that fits the department's organization. This needs explanation. Many departments can be described horizontally, in terms of the outputs of their various sections, and vertically, in terms of the processes common to all sections. Consider, for example, a hospital's laboratories. One manager may list the department's principal functions as:

- Haematology   • Chemistry   • Microbiology   • Blood Bank

But another could equally well write:

- Specimen Collection
- Testing
- Reporting
- Quality Control

It is a judgement call. And it should be the manager's since the manager is going to have to organize the QA program on the foundations of his or her principal functions.

An Ambulance Department listed its principal functions thus:

1. To provide emergency medical care and patient transfer.
2. To assist in the emergency room.
3. To assist the hospital cardiac arrest team.
4. To assist with patient portering and hard-to-handle patients.
5. To provide security.
6. To assist in maintaining the hospital grounds.

One gathers from the list of functions that ambulance drivers in this hospital are wearing at least four hats: they are drivers (patient transfer, Item 1), medics (Items 1, 3 and possibly 2), security officers (Items 4 and 5) and odd-job-men (Item 4, porters; Item 6, gardeners). Why not break out the department's role in this way:

1. To provide patient transfer services.
2. To provide or assist in emergency medical care, en route, in the emergency department and with the cardiac arrest team.
3. To act as security officers on all shifts, and
4. To provide other assistance as requested.

In all probability there will be a new item which may have been forgotten:

5. To maintain the ambulances and other outside equipment of the hospital.

Depending on the amounts of time spent on Items 4 and 5, either may fail to meet the *10 percent of role* qualifier, to be listed as a *principal* function.

People get concerned about how many principal functions there should be and in what detail they should be listed. We expect departments to list between four and six. After all, beyond Item 5 can you still call the functions you might want to list *principal* functions? Certainly any function that takes up less than 10 percent of the department's time should be questioned. If you have many discrete functions you can group them. We should remember that 20 percent of the functions will account for 80 percent of our work—the old 80:20 rule. When managers insist on going beyond five functions, I encourage them with the reminder that the QA Committee will expect them to assess on a regular basis *all* the principal functions they list. This reminder tends to cool much ardour!

2. Reporting What You Do Now

"How are you currently monitoring the quality of the work your department is doing?"

"Oh, I'm not doing any Quality Assurance yet."

"That wasn't the question. Let me put it another way: how do you know what kind of job your department is doing?"

Then, one by one as we noted in Chapter I, the untutored, but effective answers come forth: by listening to Report, inspecting the work, looking at the charts, watching the interaction, reviewing the incidents, and many more. Managers have *always* been responsible for the quality of their operation and have monitored it systematically for their own assurance and satisfaction. We are building on that given. The task here is to answer the question:

"Manager, *how* do you know?"

And managers will know by daily observation and inspection, by reviewing actual (charts, incident reports) or aggregate (number of lost-time incidents) data, and from the comments of others, clients and hospital staff, within and outside the department.

While it may appear unlikely that department heads would find it difficult to identify the means by which they are already monitoring quality, such is our experience. They have been practising quality assurance under other names and through ingrained routines so that it often takes a third party to say to them, "But doesn't that activity tell you about the *quality* of the service?" The other block is one that QA professionals like myself have put in their way. Do you remember when medicine could not do you any good unless it tasted bad? Quality assessment is like that for many managers: unless it is rigorous, formal and scientific, it can't be QA. Nonsense! The eyes, ears, touch and taste of the experienced supervisors are worth a hundred norms and criteria.

To aid in this important process of identifying current quality monitoring, there is a list at the end of this chapter of measures we have found already *in place* in hospitals, on the day we have been asked to launch their QA programs. The list is not prescriptive, nor is it in any sense complete. You may find that the lists for other departments give you ideas for your own.

We advise hospitals to call for reports on current performance as soon as possible, often within a month of the launch of the program. We also advise that each manager should report only *one* measure of performance and that he or she should report the same one for three months in succession. Some of the reasons for this have to do with the QA reporting system; others have particular relevance for department heads.

As managers begin to report their data, they are in effect going public with information which until that point they had been reviewing alone, or with their supervisors. The necessity to go public will raise a host of legitimate concerns, the answers to which should have a positive effect on the validity of the measurement and the quality awareness of the manager. Reporting is a consciousness-raising activity.

There are two developments that should occur in the department's program as a result of this initial reporting: the determination of what constitutes a QA report, and the improvement of QA measurement. We will consider them in turn.

At departmental levels, a QA report gives the answers to the following five questions:

1. What was reviewed? (topic)
2. How was it assessed? (measure)
3. What was found? (findings)
4. How is that significant? (importance) and
5. What has the department done about it? (follow-up)

The following are some examples of actual QA reports from departments:

On May 13 the Public Health Inspector visited the kitchen on his quarterly inspection. After checking all the refrigerators, store rooms, dish room, main preparation area and belt line he made two minor recommendations which were remedied before he left the premises.

or:

Unit 2 carried out a review of the Nursing Care charted in the preceding 24 hours in comparison with the Nursing Care Plan current for each patient. Thirty observations were made. The audit team (1 RN, 1 RNA) found that 90 percent of the direct care was charted but noted (a) that there were notes of patient teaching and psycho-social support on only 30 percent of the charts within the previous *seven days* and (b) that twelve of the Care Plans had not been updated during the same period. These matters were reviewed at all team conferences in the week of May 13, and a re-audit is recommended with three months.

A housekeeping inspection was carried out on May 14 covering all the public areas of the first floor; team—1 supervisor and 1 housekeeper. The overall rating according to the checklist attached was 87 percent. The results were discussed with the team on duty. One broken fixture was reported to Maintenance and the state of the floor in Admitting was brought to the attention of the manager.

In each case the paragraph explains to the layman what occurred. Where necessary, evidence is given as an attachment; such evidence may include the checklist, the criteria and actual scores on the sheet used in the audit. The intent is to limit the volume of data and, by the use of already prepared forms and lists, to limit the time spent by departments in reporting.

The second result sought from this initial series of reports is an improvement in the actual assessing. The department that assesses quality through the supervisor's random inspection needs to introduce *documentation* (who inspected what, when), then a *checklist* (what he or she was looking for), and third a *rating scale*, which can be used reliably by different raters to measure quality. Departments that have depended on management to do the assessment can use this first reporting series to involve general staff. Those with established standards and criteria will, through these assessments, have an opportunity of testing both their reliability and the usefulness of the entire measurement.

3. Planning the Department's Program

To this point in this chapter, and in the introduction of QA, everything has utilized management elements already in place: listing principal functions, identifying ways in which performance is monitored, and beginning regular reporting—but of a QA activity already being done. This introduction has served hospitals well, but now at Stage III, we counsel managers to take charge of the wheel and set a new course. In Stage III, department heads are asked to develop a plan for their QA programs.

In Chapter IV, we identified what we called the four essential components of quality assurance. These were the activities of setting objectives, promoting quality, monitoring activity, and assessing performance. We propose that department heads should plan their QA programs by taking each of their principal functions in turn and recording how they set objectives, promote quality (or intend to set, promote), etc. Exhibit 13 shows the form we encourage department heads to complete, one for each of their principal functions.

EXHIBIT 13

Quality Assurance Plan   Principal Function No. _____

Department: _____   Page: _____

Section: _____   Date: _____

To: _____

_____

_____

STANDARDS SETTING	Standards for the function are set with reference to: continued over
QUALITY PROMOTION	Quality of performance is promoted by: continued over
ACTIVITY MONITORING	The continuous execution of this function is monitored by: continued over
PERFORMANCE ASSESSMENT	The department's performance in this function is evaluated by: continued over

Exhibit 14 is the face page which identifies the department and its role, the principal functions, any current goal/MBO statements, to whom QA roles are assigned in the department, to whom the department reports, how frequently it is expected to report its program to the QA Committee, and where its QA log—or records of completed assessments—is located.

Although the forms are simple in themselves, the demands they make of the department head are exacting. It is likely that there will be many boxes left blank at the manager's first attempt to answer all the questions. That is to be expected. Our intention in Stage III is to move departments in the direction of their leading principal function, and to get that addressed effectively before moving on to other things. The other feature of the QA Plan is that it provides a flexible format that all departments can use. The collection of departmental QA Plans forms the kernel of the hospital's facility-wide outline that is demanded by the Council in its *1985 Standards*.

Let me jump to the end of the QA Planning. Department heads have worked on their principal functions one by one. Over a period of five or six months, they have logged on the form how the activities (setting . . ., promoting . . .) are increasing their sense of assurance at how well the work of each function is being done. If they then took the planning sheets for each function and lined them side by side on the desk, they would see, by the extent of the entries in each box, that different assurance activities are relevant or specifically applicable to different principal functions. What is important is that *all* functions are addressed by at least *one* assurance activity in addition to objective setting. Monitoring or assessment should be instituted as soon as a feasible way can be found but, where these are not possible, then promotional (Quality Investment) activities may have to suffice.

4. Introducing Standards and Criteria

In the fourth stage of the adult learning model, departments are called upon to start applying predetermined standards and criteria to the activity monitoring and performance assessment they are conducting and reporting. Standards and criteria are the rocks and shoals that have held fast many a QA boat and simply wrecked others and marooned their crews. For this reason, we leave until this relatively late stage the demand for their employment in the developing QA program. By this time, we reason the program is securely on the move, department heads are seeing some returns on their investment, and the request is to make more exact the measurements that are already being carried out.

Department heads are referred to Section 1 of Chapter IV, where standard setting or adoption is given full treatment. Criteria are a different matter and deserve more explanation here.

Criteria are the smallest of a hierarchy of definitions of performance. Criteria offer measurable statements by which a product or service can be judged to have met the standard set. The department says that "patient meals shall be attractive, tasty, nutritiously sound, complete and served at the correct temperature." This is a standard—or a number of them. None of the

EXHIBIT 14

Quality Assurance Plan

DEPARTMENT	Date of Origin: _____ Dates Reviewed: _____
MISSION STATEMENT	The role of the Department is to:
PRINCIPAL FUNCTIONS	1. 2. 3. 4. 5.
GOALS	The Goals of the Department were developed/last reviewed in 19 , and are attached hereto □/ stated in (reference).
QA ORGANIZATION	The department has □ has <u>no</u> □ QA Committee. The person responsible for the department's QA Program is: List Committee members: NAME TITLE
REPORTING	The Department Head reports to: (give superior's name and title) The QA Program reports to the Hospital's QA Committee: (give frequency) The Department's QA Log (of assessments and other activities) is located:

items is measurable as set down. The department's task is to turn this standard into a series of criteria. This means importing elements, i.e. criteria, against which each statement can be measured. Let's start with the easy ones first: *temperature*. The criterion might read: "The serving temperature of each item on the tray shall fall within the ranges set out in the 1979 *Dietetic Department Guidelines in Smaller Health Care Facilities* (published by National Health and Welfare, p.30)." More simply, the criteria might list the various ranges, thus:

1. Broth, soups and hot beverages shall be served at a temperature between 82°–88°C (or 170°–190°F);
2. Meat, portioned for serving . . . (etc.)

The criteria for *nutritiously sound* would probably make reference to Canada's Food Guide and the advisability of including a good variety of food groups in the total meal. By *complete*, the department will likely mean that the delivered tray shall contain *all* the items listed on the menu checked by or for the patient, and *all* the kitchenware and condiments set for that meal according to the department's procedure manual. Thus, the criteria for this requirement are, first, the menu itself, and second, the picture/list/diagram of the complete tray. *Attractive* and *tasty* are adjectives that depend on subjective appraisal. They depend on my judgement or your judgement, and of course we might not agree, particularly if we had differing ethnic backgrounds. With important but subjective standards like attractiveness and tastiness, we can not use criteria. Instead, we have to broaden the audit and include a panel of appraisers, each of whom would be asked to give a rating to a limited number of questions: the attractiveness of the tray's total appearance, the presentation and visual appeal of the main dishes, their taste, texture, quantities, and variety.

5. Quality Assurance in Nursing

Integrating the Nursing Department into the hospital-wide program has raised special, but not unanticipated, problems. I want to address four—the scale of the department, principal functions in nursing, performance assessment, and the use of the nursing audit.

5.1. Department Scale

In comparison with other hospital departments, nursing is both large in employees and budget and very varied in its activity. For reasons of size and organization, nursing departments have usually chosen to establish their own QA Committees to coordinate the QA programs of their general and special units, rather than have them report independently to the hospital's QA Committee. This has had three obvious benefits: first, general in-patient units have been able to work together on various elements of the program rather than each one having to do original work. Second, Nursing QA Committees have taken a burden off the hospital committee without lessening either its authority or its opportunity to evaluate the audits and programs existing at unit level. Third, Nursing Audit Committees, which are in place in most medium-to-large hospitals, can be given a more comprehensive role as QA Committees and a legitimate function in the hospital-wide program.

5.2. Principal Functions

It has usually been difficult for head nurses and their superiors to fit professional nursing into the categories used in the adult learning model. The nursing process is intentionally not divisible. Rather, it is a single, problem-solving cycle, beginning with:

- Data gathering;
- Assessment, including the identification of problems/nursing diagnosis;
- Planning of care;
- Nursing intervention; and
- Evaluation,

which picks up the cycle again.

Although nursing departments will seldom want to base audits on a single step in the cycle, there is merit in listing the five steps as nursing's principal functions. They set out, in the profession's own terms, what its members are doing and how.

5.3. Performance Assessment

The concurrent nursing audit is the classic vehicle for assessing the performance of the nurse and the nursing process. It treats the process as a whole and it looks at all the data available on the patient—retrospective and concurrent—and the patient in the bed. Its scale raises certain problems, which are addressed below. But nursing performance can also be assessed with reference to structure and outcome. Following are some examples of assessments of structure:

- **Nursing credentials**—registration, certifications, continuing education and performance appraisal;
- **Nurse staffing**—the application and validation of workload management systems;
- **Equipment and environment issues**—audits of the biomedical equipment and the safety and convenience of the environment for patients and staff.

Both in Canada and the U.S., QA is moving towards the assessment of clinical outcome. Data can be negative, e.g., incidents, accidents and complaints. But they can be positive too. With a concurrent monitoring system the *absence* of incidents spells reliability. There is also the possibility of showing the coincidence of specific and beneficial outcome with care plans that specify the same outcome as the goal of chosen interventions.

5.4. The Nursing Audit

Before leaving the special problems our implementation poses for nursing departments, I must answer a question left hanging by my earlier prescriptions: "We have spent a minimum of three years getting our Concurrent Audit in shape. Are you suggesting that we abandon it completely?" The fourth question specific to nursing concerns the relevance of the nursing audit systems already in place. When QA standards were first put on the table in Canada in March, 1983, most people thought that with their current audit systems both medicine and nursing were thoroughly in compliance with the Council's requirements. Increasingly, both have realized that QA was more than a new vocabulary; it was calling for quite new forms of performance review. Not only was QA more than audit, but it occurred to some that audit might be an inefficient way of evaluating performance.

The outsider gets two impressions of pre-QA nursing audits from nursing management. First is a sense of pride in what the department has developed. Audits are admired for their scope and detail. But, second, one is impressed at how expensive they are, both in their heavy development cost and in their application. Estimates vary as to the time it takes to carry out a thorough audit of a single patient. I have heard a range of answers, from 40 minutes to an hour and a half. Usually training is required of those who are to use the audit form. This concern about expense is often voiced in the question "How many do we have to do?" But there is a more serious problem.

Nursing Audit is the correct answer to the 1977 Council demand, but it does not fit the 1983 or the 1985 *Standards* except by adaptation. In the 1985 *Standards*, the Council is asking for the establishment of goals, the implementation of procedures to meet those goals, the measurement of performance against goals, and the introduction of remedies to meet the discrepancies discovered. Nursing Audit tends to give a mass of information about the care received by individual patients, but not enough information about the care provided to a mass of patients, for the nursing department to make statements about its level of practice, or for Unit A to identify common deficiencies. Few hospitals are able to do *enough* comprehensive audits to demonstrate specific competence or deficiency.

There is, however, a relatively simple solution. Our instructions have been:

- *Select one section* of the comprehensive nursing audit *and apply it* to 20-25 percent of the patients on each unit, during one or two weeks. Analyze the data, draw your conclusions, introduce improvements, set a date for re-audit, and report. Next month, take another section of the Audit protocol and follow the same routine.

In one hospital they decided to look at the handling of intravenous therapy which was part of the "medications" section. The Audit Committee chose to review *all* of the current in-patient IVs. As a result of these audits, each of which took no more than ten minutes, it was established that whereas on two surgical units IVs were quite well handled, on the third, staff exhibited a range of problems. This information made remedial action easy to target and specific in application.

- *Review and revise the audit section before and after use.* Our second word of advice deals with the common experience of finding a questionnaire inadequate for the user's current interests. When a section is lifted from a whole audit it has to be augmented to make it free-standing, but often auditors need to tailor it so that it will be comprehensive and specific enough to constitute an adequate test of the care under review. Our advice is to augment it before and leave notes *after* administration, to show how it should be improved before its next use. We suggest that no more than once a year the Audit Committee should review the entire audit and at that time incorporate *all* the changes. In this way the hospital will always have a tested and current audit protocol.

Those who think spatially will see that while we have left the concurrent Nursing Audit intact, we have changed its mode of application from vertical (all the elements of Mrs. Jones' care) to horizontal (the Recovery Room care of Mrs. Jones and all [or 20%] of the other patients). The merits of this strategy are (1) reliable conclusions, (2) ease of application, (3) satisfaction with the audit process, (4) serial review of all elements of care and (5) regular up-dating of the whole protocol.

6. The Feasibility of Quality Assurance

Managers find the description of the many demands of a QA program quite threatening. Many are worried by the program's complexity, and nearly everyone about the time it will require. "Am I expected to be Supermanager? However am I going to be able to do all this?" they wonder silently, as they listen to the account of the new, wonderful program.

The adult learning model has been successful because it is a feasible program for working supervisors, charge technologists and therapists, not just for department heads who are full-time managers. Implementation of QA is expected to be done alongside and secondary to the supervisor's principal functions. We have designed a series of manageable steps through which a simple but effective program can be grown. But how does the manager keep going? If the Head Nurse was juggling three balls in the air before QA, how many have we added? Perhaps we have just substituted heavier objects of different sizes which she is still expected to keep moving in the air.

I do not want in this section to suggest that the QA task is small, nor insult managers by suggesting that they are not really as busy as they complain. QA is a major endeavour, and managers who are worth their salt are already having to make choices as to how they spend their time, and how much work they take home with them. I have four words of advice which may fit different people and situations: sharing, sampling, mileage, and As and Cs. These obviously need explanation.

6.1. Sharing

If managers can buy the proposal that QA is a staff activity, and are not threatened by admitting that their personal knowledge of QA is not much better than that of their subordinates, sharing may be a logical way to begin and continue QA. Managers can say to themselves and then to their staff: QA is not a job particularly for me, QA is, like the nursing process, the way in which we deliver care or service; it is a shared responsibility to discover this process and follow it to the improvement of care and the maintenance of quality.

I have indicated that all segments of the QA process, except reporting, are appropriate to staff participation. Practitioners can have a part in the process of adoption of the department's care or service goals. Staff should help develop, adapt or refine the standards of performance they must meet. Certainly they should play a major role in quality control, performance monitoring and assessment. When audits are required, they should be involved in the development of the protocol, the measurement, analysis of data and the search for effective remedies.

6.2. Sampling

A friend said of an elderly relative: "I don't think she has ever had a thought that she has not expressed, more than once." People are like that with QA. They want to write standards for everything, quantify everything, and then report *all* their data. But these are impossible and ludicrous goals. Only significant data should be reported; just enough measurement should be done to establish a conclusion; and standards should not be written where performance goals are more appropriate, and where appraisals depend on subjective judgement. The advice is that department heads should apply the tests of appropriateness and significance and remember to measure only a fraction (sample) of the whole and look at enough occasions (frequency) to draw conclusions.

6.3. Mileage

Mileage is to the manager what leverage is to the investor, a basic strategy for getting the biggest bang for the buck. The strategy of getting the most mileage out of a piece of work stimulates the manager to make the same basic effort count for more than one purpose. Consulting firms regularly use new projects as opportunities to (1) earn revenue, (2) develop the skills of their junior staff, (3) package new solutions for later clients, and (4) as subjects for marketing literature and fresh ingredients for proposals. It is unlikely that managers will get four products out of one endeavour, but they should get two uses out of all substantial work, and must get in the habit of looking for the second application. Some examples:

- Incorporate within the department's QA program appraisals of the department carried out by others;

- Use the standards developed for an audit as the basis for revising and updating policy and procedure manuals;
- Document in a single paragraph existing routines that support or monitor quality; and
- Make monthly statistical and financial information part of the QA report, stressing elements of quality, productivity or management control.

6.4. As and Cs

Alan Lakein's *How to Get Control of Your Time and Your Life* (New York: Signet, 1974) is my time management bible. You should read it too. Basic to his system of getting control of our time is the instruction to make a daily list of things to be done *and* to rank that list in terms of As, really important tasks, Bs, of medium importance and Cs, incidental activities. His next instruction is, of course, do As first, then Bs, and don't bother with Cs. But, if you are like me, you do Cs, masses of them. Meanwhile, the As don't get done. When I am managing my time, I do As and I have two experiences: first, that the As shrink when tackled resolutely and are seldom as big as they look; and second, if I don't do the Cs, someone else does—they do themselves, or they just go away! Yes, QA is going to mean more work, more As, perhaps more delegated As and more Cs *neglected*, pushed out of our days by the more insistent tasks which really should demand our attention.

7. Continuous Evolution

One of the fundamental contentions of this book is that QA programs should be grown rather than built from the flat earth. We are equally certain that a QA program is not a building, but an organism. Buildings do not change; for better or worse, they remain, until added to, forcibly converted or pulled down. An organism always has within its existence the forces of death and decay and those of life and regeneration. This is quality assurance. If performance is unmonitored and studies repeated without correction or improvement, decay and deterioration will set in. If better standards are developed, measures are improved and problems identified and solved, life, excitement and reward will be part of that program. But QA and QA programs have never finally arrived. There will never come a time when those in charge can relax and let them run themselves. When this happens, the force of decay is given the opportunity for ascendency. Fortunately, while there are many satisfactions along the way, there are few occasions when profound self-congratulation is possible. Our measurements are partial, our assessment of outcomes often unsatisfying, and our need for vigilance constant.

The prospect of continuous evolution could be seen as an intolerable future, a never-stopping treadmill. Alternatively, department heads can take courage from the knowledge that if they start where they are, they will have the opportunity of improving both performance and its measurement. This opportunity will occur because of two elements intrinsic to QA: QA is an auto-tutorial activity, that is, by doing it, one learns how to do it better. Second, QA is a shared endeavour in which peers, superiors and subordinates play roles that support and encourage the manager's leadership. QA is a new style of hospital management. It promises to be the integrating factor in all the administrative roles the manager is called upon to play.

EXHIBIT 15

Quality Monitors in Place

A. Finance
Monthly operating statements for CEO and Finance Committee
Daily/weekly/monthly reconciliation of accounts
Annual and bi-annual audit including management letter
Payroll accuracy (× 2 weeks)
Audit of master file system

B. Personnel
Recruitment audit—speed, appropriateness
Benefit enrollment
Audit of hospital-wide performance appraisal program
Employment Standards Act audit
Analysis of union grievances

C. Medical Records
Monthly count of incomplete charts
Complaints of charts not available
Audits on transcription/chart deficiencies/coding and abstracting techniques
External audit—HMRI

D. Admitting
Concurrent audit of admitting procedure (random sample)
Audit of accuracy of A/D/T lists
Assessment of discharge/transfer system

E.1. Occupational Health and Safety
Audit of Workers' Compensation Board Claims
Safety inspections, weekly/monthly
Ministry of Labour inspections
Investigation of employee incidents and lost-time accidents

2. Infection Control
Investigation of reported infections
Analysis of hospital-acquired and community-acquired infections
Audit of aseptic procedures
Sterilizer monitoring

F. Staff education
Program evaluations/list of program attendance
Competency-based evaluation/program effectiveness—based on incidents
Recertification of delegated acts

G. Psychology
Chart audit
Audit of psychological assessment reports
Workload analysis: direct vs. indirect care hours

H. Engineering
Record of breakdowns
Quality of air (winter)
Boiler efficiency (percentage)
Heating system efficiency (percentage)
Testing of emergency power
Chemical treatment of water system

I. Maintenance
Preventative maintenance program
Monitoring maintenance requisition system
Weekly inspections
Ontario Hydro random inspections of new work
External inspections

J. Materials Management
Reconciliation of purchase
requisitions to receipts
(weekly)
Client satisfaction survey
Weekly inventory control (stock
level check)
Audit of follow-up requests
Audit of quota system

K. Housekeeping
Weekly inspection
Monitoring pest control contract

L. Dietetics and Food Services
Nutritional audits (retro. chart)
Menu audit
Tray audit
Tray returns (therapeutic diets)
Patient satisfaction
questionnaires/interviews
Accuracy of food production
scheduling
Sanitation inspections, daily
Public Health inspection of
kitchen
New food evaluation
Temperature checks
Trayline assessments

M. Social Work
Case book audits (retro. chart
audit)
Peer review audit
Patient satisfaction survey

N. Chaplaincy
Review of on-call activity
Review of numbers (1) at
worship; (2) in counselling
Reports of education programs
for external students/pastors

O. Physiotherapy
Patient outcomes: comparison of
status on admission and
discharge
Health status rating forms
Chart audit (retro.) (1)
documentation; (2) patient care
Patient questionnaires

P. Occupational Therapy
COTA accreditation for OT
student placement

Q. Fire Preparedness
Monthly fire drill/standby drills
Monthly monitoring of fire
equipment and alarm systems
Biennial external inspection: fire
marshal's office

R. Radiology
MOH radiation protection branch
inspections
Reject/repeat rates
Accuracy and timeliness of
report/audit of dictation
Audit of patient waiting time
Spot check on film library
Outages/breakdowns
Dose measurement
Check on automatic processor
Monthly statistics

S. Laboratories
LPTP (Laboratory Proficiency
Testing Program)
Incidents—reported internally
and by external department
Turnaround times
Lab orders
Quality control data
Preventative maintenance control
MD and patient surveys

T. Pharmacy
Errors in dispensing
Delays in dispensing
Weekly inspection—in pharmacy
and/or units—and restocking
Narcotic controls
Drug utilization review

U. Nursing
Concurrent nursing audit
Nursing practice standards
Analysis of incidents, quarterly
Nursing workload management
system: consistency and
appropriateness
Mini-audits:
Documentation of response to
PRN medications
Documentation of patient
teaching and response
Nursing histories (completion)
Nursing care plans (currency)

CHAPTER VI

The Measurement of Quality

People who have helped others begin their QA programs will be familiar with the typical confusion that surrounds the measurement of quality. Beginners must cope with assorted terms, norms, standards and criteria, structures, processes and outcomes, audits and peer reviews, raw scores and percentages. Often they must cope with value judgements that are not helpful—favouring audits, percentages, standards, and outcomes over observations, goals, quality control, and process. For the beginner, there seem to be all too few easy or simple ways to plan and carry out a basic assessment of the department's performance. These perceptions led me to write a paper, "The Measurement of Quality," which later became Chapter II of *Quality Assurance: Getting Started* (OHA, 1985). This paper described a simple process and set out various options that need to be considered in sequence in the planning of a quality assessment. The response to that chapter has been very gratifying. It seems to have met a need, the need for a simple jargon-free series of steps and choices in doing the central task of QA: measuring quality. Perhaps, also, the chapter validated some subjective means of assessment that their practitioners had felt were somehow inferior. In this present chapter, we will present the same process with some additional explorations and some further refinements.

The important point to stress is that the Quality Assessment process is a planning model for quality appraisal, and not just a listing of variables.

1. Choosing the Principal Function

Choosing the principal function is the essential first step in quality assessment. Quality assessment is something one does in respect of principal functions, and those functions alone. Also, one assesses those functions with a frequency appropriate to their rank. Over time, principal function No. 1 will be assessed more frequently than any other; No. 2 next, and so on. A colleague of mine likes to tell the following story to warn people what not to do in his field, which is research.

A man was walking home late one night from a party in the neighbourhood, when he saw a man on his hands and knees by a lamp post.

"What are you doing, my good man?" asked the first.

"I am looking for my car keys," replied the man on his knees.

"Where did you lose them?" asked the first, about to join in the search.

"Over there," replied the other, pointing some way down the tree-lined sidewalk.

"Well then, why are we looking here?" asked the first.

"Well, this is where the light is," answered the former owner of the keys.

There is always the danger in QA of assessing activities and people and systems just because they are easily accessible and assessable—and not because they deserve assessment, on their own merits. There is one exception. When beginning a program, we do—and think it is helpful to—ask department heads to report data from a quality measurement they are *already* engaged in, regardless of its reference to a principal function.

2. Focus of Inquiry

The Quality Assessment Model details four more questions where answers in succession will create a practical assessment plan: focus, expectations, methods, and judgement. These questions are:

What are you going to look at? (The question of focus)
What are you going to look for? (Expectations)
How are you going to look? (The question of method)
How do you know what good looks like? (The validity of the appraisals being made).

We are all indebted to Donabedian for helping us see that quality can be appraised, even when we cannot use outcomes as the measure of our performance. And, of course, that is so often the case in human service work. Not only are *outcomes* difficult to measure, but their accurate attribution to the efforts of individuals or teams, particular departments or sometimes even specific therapeutic interventions (operation, treatments, medications) is quite impossible. Under these conditions, Donabedian advises us of the availability of secondary questions. We can look at inputs or what he calls *structure*. These include people, equipment, and the environment. We can also focus on the ways things are done, and the ways care is given. Donabedian calls this element *process* (Donabedian, 1980).

A total of six elements of a principal function that could be the focus of a quality assessment were listed in *Quality Assurance: Getting Started*. The list today stands at eight:

1. *Goals* or objectives
2. *Structure* 2.1 People
          2.2 Equipment
          2.3 Environment

3. *Process*, methods or procedures
4. *Outcome* 4.1 Quantity
   4.2 Quality
   4.3 Client Satisfaction

2.1. Goals

Generally, goals are what performance is measured *against*; but goals can themselves be assessed against an appropriate standard:

2.1.1 The board may wish to review the adequacy of the hospital's mission statement against the standards laid out (*Standard* I: Mission Statement, Goals, Objectives and Planning, p.2, 1985) by CCHA in the section on Governing Body and Administration.

2.1.2 Nursing care plans and treatment plans of other disciplines are future-oriented, and contain performance goals for patient and staff. These are assessable, and well worth assessing.

2.1.3 Annually, every hospital must draw up and submit an operating budget. This can be assessed as a planning document. Does it demonstrate an underlying fiscal strategy for the hospital? Have resources been allocated within the hospital in a manner sensitive to its objectives and the cost centres' ability to cope with their volumes?

2.2. Structure or Inputs

2.2.1 People. When the accreditation process was first organized, there was the realization that outside surveyors could not make valid judgements on the quality of the care itself, so its judgements were based on the simple model, which states that good care is a product of the right *people* carrying out the best *procedures* in a safe *environment*.

People are the first ingredient in this equation. Their quality as a component would include *numbers*—enough staff; *qualifications*—the right mix of professional and non-professional staff; and *competence*—people with current and demonstrable skills. QA tends to look at the third of these aspects, perhaps in part because it does not want to take on the financial/political issues, a not inappropriate reluctance. While Administration may itself use QA data to determine where extra resources are needed, it will respond negatively to those who would use the QA process simply for financial leverage.

Instead, quality assessment, as it is applied to people, will focus on the competence aspect:

- Medical staff credentials: how are privileges granted and reviewed? are they ever limited or withdrawn?
- Delegated medical acts: are nurses expected to perform appropriate duties? are they requalified annually?

- Emergencies: what percentage of MDs, RNs, other health professionals, administration and general staff are qualified in CPR?
- Continuing education: how is annual performance appraisal administered? What standards does the hospital/department have for continuing education and competence testing in newly recruited staff?

These are some examples of appropriate questions that can be asked and answered satisfactorily in a quality assessment review.

2.2.2 Equipment.

Hospitals are inevitable arsenals of equipment and supplies, both of which fall within this category. Equipment runs the gamut from the heavy boilers in the power house to the electronic implanted cardiac pacemaker. All of them fall within the purview of QA because their safe and reliable functioning is essential to the hospital and the patient care it provides. But QA will discriminate between what it requires in a machine; reliability and efficiency may be the chief attributes of a gross motor, whereas safety and accuracy may be of primary concern in clinical equipment.

In certain departments, supplies are a more critical component than equipment. Two departments that come to mind immediately are pharmacy and food services. Meanwhile nursing, with its heavy usage of medical-surgical supplies, would have much to oversee through its QA program. The point to be made here is that equipment and supplies are neither unimportant components in the equation of care, nor are they inaccessible to quality assurance.

2.2.3 Environment.

In their environment, patients and staff ask for (1) safety, (2) comfort, and (3) good housekeeping. Safety is the critical element; the environment needs to be free of hazards that might cause damage by infection, application (noxious gases and other substances), or trauma. This is where the hospital's Occupational Health and Safety program comes into its own. It monitors accident statistics, it investigates incidents, injuries and hazards, it recommends and follows up on remedial action, and it submits its program and results to the scrutiny of two or three outside agencies.

By "comfort," we are referring to environmental controls of heat and cold, humidity and air quality. "Good housekeeping" means a whole lot more than cleanliness. It also refers to the restfulness and attractiveness of decor and furnishings. Of course, environmental conditions are far easier to monitor than is the attractiveness of the hospital's decor, and more can be done about them. The time to monitor and assess the attractiveness of decor is *before* the colours are chosen or the floor or furniture covering is purchased.

2.3. Methods or Procedures

These elements are *process*, the way things are done and what is done in given situations. If we cannot tell, the argument goes, what are the results of a specific intervention, then we can pass judgement on whether it was the correct intervention in the circumstances or whether the process itself was done correctly. In the one case, we are comparing the discretion of the clinician with the collective wisdom of other clinicians; in the other, we are reviewing the skill with which the procedure was carried out. The clinical audit cycle (see Chapter II) is a process review, and not the scientific peer review of outcome. In one sense *process* is second best as a focus of assessment, but it has many merits of its own. It is fairer to clinicians; it reviews their work on the basis of the knowledge that was available to them at the time. It respects the therapeutic resources available; it does not demand the same high technology care in, say, a small rural hospital that it would appropriately expect at a big-city teaching hospital. And the review can be conducted with more objectivity than can a death review, for example, in which 20:20 hindsight and the practitioner's need to minimize his or her responsibility take precedence over clinical insight.

If process review is valid for the physician, then it certainly is for others whose clinical discretion is under review, as it is also for those whose skill is being assessed. The other important note is that the subject of process review is not a single person or a single procedure, but multiples of both. QA is the creation, monitoring and assessment of systems: that is, many people doing the same things repeatedly to established standards. Thus, the assessment judges the effectiveness of the system and not the skill of named individuals.

2.4. Outcome

As indicated, outcome can be reviewed in three ways: productivity, quality, and client satisfaction.

2.4.1 Productivity. The inclusion of productivity—the number of widgets—in a treatise on quality may occasion some surprise. The assumption is that QA is concerned with the character of the widgets themselves, how well they meet the specifications laid down for them. But that attitude is somewhat naive. There is first a hidden assumption that quantity and quality are inversely related—high quality goes with low productivity. This is hardly defensible in an age that mass produces products of very high quality. Secondly, we have to acknowledge that cost and volume of output are part of the same equation of effective management as is the quality of the goods and services produced. When administration and hospital boards compare departmental statistics with those of similar departments in their hospital's peer group, they are looking at the quality of their operation.

Productivity is taken for quality in, for example, the power plant where boiler efficiency (litres or cubic metres of fuel to the quantity of heat produced) and the efficiency of the heating system (volume of raw water added to that circulating) are decidedly notions of quality. Medical Records is concerned about output (in numbers of lines of transcription) and turn-around time. Discharge planners satisfy patients, families, physicians and the hospital by securing early placement. Of course, productivity is a mark of quality for the fund-raiser. But it is also true for the Director of Volunteers: how many he or she is able to recruit, place and retain. In a long-term facility, it would be fair to judge the effectiveness of the recreational program in part by the number of different activities sponsored and, more important, the number of different patients who had been involved in them.

2.4.2 Quality. This is the most desirable focus in a quality assessment of all the eight alternatives listed in this section. The intention in the assessment is to ask how good, or how effective, was the product or service achieved by my department or team. We have indicated that it is seldom feasible to measure quality of outcome in a hospital. This is true for clinical programs because of the difficulties noted above—those of measuring changes in a patient's condition and of attributing measured changes to individual interventions. However, it is not true of other aspects of hospital work. We can measure the cleanliness of a room, the accuracy of accounts and abstracts (in Medical Records) and the effective learning (behaviour change) of budget skills, fire preparedness, CPR and all manner of clinical skills. In fact, there is hardly a department that cannot point to some element of its work, whose quality of outcome can appropriately be assessed.

2.4.3 Client Satisfaction. Client satisfaction is listed as an outcome distinct from productivity and quality because in a human service enterprise, the client's perception of the product or service is both very important and *not* always related to the standards chiefly respected by the professional. For example, the care on the unit may have been sloppy in the extreme with missed treatments, poor charting, late consultations, and wrong medications, but the patient's perception was that he was receiving excellent and sympathetic care. We would treat that perception as another element of quality. We choose not to compare the one with the other, and reserve the term quality for what is validated by professional standards.

The term client is used to refer to patients and families, but also other consumers of the department's care or service, such as other departments in the hospital. For example: Medical Records is a client of Admitting, Nursing of Housekeeping, everyone of Materials Management, physicians of Nursing, Radiology, Labs and so forth. There will be times when it is appropriate for one department to call for the assessment of their level of service by one or more client departments.

3. Stating Expectations

Quality assessment is not just lifting the lid to see what is cooking. It should be a well-planned endeavour in which the inquirer is clear what is being sought. Academic researchers have scorn for those of their colleagues who "go off on a fishing expedition" to see what is there, instead of setting up hypotheses or predictions and testing their accuracy. So too with quality assessment: we should not think highly of people who want just to fumble about in the records or charts to see what is there. In the first place, the department head or supervisor should be close enough to the action to have appropriate questions on which to base a focussed assessment. In the second, some broad-brush inquiries yield such variety of data that their significance is unclear and appropriate responses to them difficult or impossible.

Accordingly, we support the QA professionals who call for the use of stated goals, standards and criteria, as the essential *structure* of quality assessment. You can think of them as another lens that provides a tighter focus than the alternatives given in our last section. Having decided to base an assessment on the *procedures*—for example, of principal function No. 2—the assessor in this step will define the characteristics of the procedure as she would want it to be demonstrated by the staff in her department.

We have used three terms: goals, standards, and criteria. All of them have been discussed quite extensively in previous chapters: goals and standards are the first of our four essential components of QA in Chapter IV and criteria in Section 4 of the last chapter on implementing QA in the department. It is worth repeating the simple introduction given to standards and criteria in *Quality Assurance: Getting Started*.

> The (next) question in the assessment process is the determination of *what the inquirer is looking for.* Answers come in two kinds: *quantitative* (Is something there? If so, how much of it/how many of them?) and *qualitative* (Is what is there of the right kind or condition?)
>
> *Quantities* in quality assessment need to be related to set expectations, and *quality* to the principal properties of the ideal product or service. These expectations, attainments and desired characteristics we call *standards* and *criteria.*
>
> These words, "standards" and "criteria" are often used interchangeably in QA, with the speaker often insisting that his or her usage alone is correct. For clarity of communication, hospitals should insist on one usage for each word among their staff. In this paper, *standard* means "a plain statement of performance" as will be found in the *Standards for Accreditation of Canadian Health Care Facilities.* The word *criterion* here is reserved for "a measurable aspect of desired performance." Criteria will either prescribe that something will, *or will not*, be found on examination, or will be found in a set quantity or within a set time. Each criterion should include or imply a number (none/all) with which the observation can be compared. Beginners should not be intimidated by the jargon and myth of QA. Standards are just expectations or requirements—what did you want/were you looking for? And criteria are the answers to the question: what is 100 percent (OHA, p.12, 1985)?

Exhibit 16 lists do's and don'ts for setting standards and criteria.

Before leaving this third question: What to look for?, I want to vote in favour of articulating goals or targets for performance. Standards and criteria are popular with QA professionals as a basis for assessment, because of their exactness—all or nothing, 0 percent or 100 percent. But what happens when these standards are scarcely attainable or when there is no set maximum? There is a tendency to want to fudge: 100 percent is the standard, but in fact 70 percent is acceptable and 80 percent is an excellent target. Often it is put the other way: the standard is *no* lost-time injuries/medication incidents, but

EXHIBIT 16

Developing Standards and Criteria: Seven Do's and Dont's

1. Don't write standards *until* you plan to use them.

2. Never develop new standards *when* you can adapt them from somewhere else (CCHA standards, Policy and Procedure Manuals, etc.).

3. Write standards by answering the questions: What am I looking for? What does "good" look like?

4. Always write standards before you do an assessment/audit/observation.

5. Always revise and add to your standards after you have done an assessment/audit/observation.

6. Involve staff in developing standards for the work they do.

7. Remember your standards and criteria should RUMBA. That is, they should be:

   - Relevant
   - Understandable
   - Measurable
   - Behavioural
   - Achievable

we have never been below 10 to 20 per month since we began keeping records. In both cases, however, informally we have acquiesced in a goal. It is preferable to establish the target in advance, often with reference to other hospitals or departments. Then the actual results can be compared with an agreed goal.

4. Method of Inquiry

In spite of the multiplicity of names given to the review, appraisal, assessment, audit, inquiry, and evaluation of quality, care, program, practice, standards and process, there are a limited number—we suggest four—generic methods of inquiry. They differ in complexity and in their timing relative to the care/service being evaluated.

4.1. Recording the Numbers

The simplest method of inquiry is the recognition and plotting of numbers that occur in a sequence. In a recent *New Yorker* cartoon, a company president is pointing to a profit and loss graph on the wall. The line representing the company's record has gone off the bottom of the chart after many periods of much higher performance. "No, Mr. Harbuttle," the president is saying to a bespectacled young man, "that does not say that the company enjoyed a good third quarter."

Our point exactly: many numbers when recorded against last quarter, budget, or confidence ranges tell their own story immediately. We may not know why they are positive or negative, but their display renders a clear judgement on the performance of a human or mechanical system.

Hospitals in many provinces use the quarterly Hospital Information System (HIS or QHIS) statistics as a barometer of their performance by department. The finance department will have many figures that reflect on the performance of the hospital, individual departments and the accounting function itself. In addition, most departments have their own domestic statistics that they use as a bellwether. Examples have been given already. At the risk of repetition, here are some common indicators: *Laboratory*—Laboratory Proficiency Testing Program (LPTP) results; *Radiology*—film re-take rates; *Medical Records*—number of delinquent charts; *Pharmacy*—number of dispensing, etc. errors/non-formulary drugs ordered; *Materials management*—many statistics around inventories, out-of-stock items and delays in acquisitions; *Personnel*—sickness and absentee rates, employee turnover, and delays in recruitment.

Many statistics are already an integral part of the departments' quality control or monitoring program. Some are generated by the machine doing the job—word processor, plant equipment, or electronic device. Other numbers are accumulated through daily returns and analyzed by computer. Our advice to department heads is to use in QA whatever numerical data are available to them. Few statistics are exciting.

4.2. Inspecting the Work

Inspections are always concurrent, which means that they mostly fall within our category of *activity monitoring* rather than performance assessment. Inspections may just as well be performed by peers in the quality review system (safety inspection, or film quality control in radiology) as by the supervisor. Inspections are always sensory, that is, involving eyes, ears, hands and sometimes taste and smell. And they are satisfying to carry out for three reasons; inspections deal with primary data—the event itself, rather than the record of the event. Second, there is often the opportunity of applying a remedy, an improvement, immediately. Third, the practitioner's learning is enhanced because the commendation or correction occurs within the immediate context of his or her performance.

4.3. Reviewing Charts and Records

Most performance assessment depends on the analysis of retrospective data. These analyses present at least two advantages over working with concurrent material. Many more data can be examined in more detail at the time of the audit, and more people can be engaged in the review and analysis than could be involved in a concurrent review. Retrospective data are found primarily in patient charts, but the analyses of incidents and events is important for the discernment of patterns of negative occurrence. Maintenance requisitions may well tell the story about equipment that is failing. Multiple events brought to the attention of the chief of staff or service chief may trigger a thorough review of a surgeon's privileges. Treatment records in rehabilitation may show important variations in the durations of treatment and use of treatment modalities between practitioners, which should be brought to their attention. These are some examples of data available to department heads *outside* of health records, whose analysis would be important in performance assessment, and in remedial action/problem solving.

In performance evaluation, the assessor reviews records with a criteria list in his or her hand. Is there a record of the following interventions in this patient's chart? What negative data are present, such as repeat service calls on equipment? In medical audit, the Health Record Administrator will be reviewing a designated number of same-disease charts to compare actual treatments/orders with criteria recently adopted by the relevant medical department. Physical medicine, psycho-social departments and nursing all rely heavily on chart audits.

4.4. Asking for Opinions

We are looking at two quite different modes of inquiry under this heading: investigation and client satisfaction. The investigation of an incident or succession of them is an important management responsibility. Investigation is necessary because incidents seldom come with all the data required for accurate determination of course, or choice of appropriate remedy. Often additional information will come from other staff or patients.

In Section 2.8 above, we identified client satisfaction as a form of *outcome* that could be reviewed in quality assessment. Our task here is to say how such data can be derived—whatever their validity. Patients can be asked to complete questionnaires, report to staff through structured interviews or answer telephone questions in their homes following discharge. The last method is used least frequently, but it may yield the most reliable data. The patient is outside the anxiety net of the hospital; the interviewer can ask direct questions and limit the halo effect by asking for specific events.

Earlier in the chapter, we expressed caution over validity of patient information and reminded readers that other departments were often clients, with reliable information on the service levels of the inquiring department.

5. Making Judgements

The last step in the planning of quality assessment is the determination of who shall say what quality has been achieved in the performance under scrutiny. For such judgements to have any validity, they must be more than the subjective appraisal of one person. In this section we discuss five alternatives, some of which overlap.

5.1. An External Agency

Hospitals, as we have already had cause to note, are subject to inspection and appraisal by a wide variety of governmental and non-governmental agencies.

Generally speaking, health-care facilities have learned to accept such appraisals and even welcome them, because of the sense of security they bring. The almost universal acceptance of and participation in the accreditation program—a *voluntary* program—is evidence of their general positive attitude. Quality judgements by external agencies are welcome in QA for three reasons: (1) they appeal to trustees, the community and other external agencies; (2) the reviewing agency conducts its appraisal in the context of hundreds of other similar appraisals, i.e. they are competently done for the most part; and (3) they apply their own standards that should have been thoroughly tested.

5.2. Res Ipsa Loquitur

Res ipsa loquitur or, literally, "the thing speaks for itself"—is a Latin tag used by lawyers to say that something is self-evident. In the Watergate inquiry, people were looking for what they called "the smoking gun" that would connect Richard Nixon undeniably with the burglary of the Democratic National Headquarters, and the subsequent cover-up. If standards and criteria are tightly set—that is, with focus and clear definition—when the performance records are compared with the desired (and defined) behaviour, the thing speaks for itself. The criteria state:

> "There shall be a written history and physical on all charts within 24 hours of admission."
> "Was it there or wasn't it?"
> "Well I had dictated it, but it was Saturday evening and medical records does not transcribe over the weekend."
> "Excuse me, was it there or wasn't it?"
> Res ipsa loquitur!

Game over. The question admits of only two answers, 0 and 1, and not "The cheque is in the mail." To repeat, if you write your standards and criteria exactly, special judgements will have to be made in less than 5 percent of cases where a truly unusual situation has occurred, one that defies the standards. In medical audit, the audit committee aims to write its standards so tightly that it becomes a semi-mechanical task for a health record administrator to determine whether the standards have been met or not. The review/investigation of exceptions or outliers is then returned to the physician members of the committee.

5.3. Peers

Mention of medical audit introduces the whole topic of peer review, since the latter is an essential feature in all medical quality assurance. Peers can be involved in quality assessment at two stages: in standards setting and in the inquiry itself. The inquiry may mean the special examination of cases that did not meet the standards or it may involve the peer in the concurrent assessment of performance. The involvement of peers in concurrent assessment, while quite rare for physicians, is common for other disciplines, particularly those whose records are inadequate for assessment purposes. The assessment of teaching programs, counselling skills, group work, cleanliness and even patient care may all be better observed by peers than derived from records.

The use of peers as assessors is preferable to management appraisal for three reasons: (1) practitioner appraisal may be more accurate than appraisals carried out by those who no longer do the task being reviewed; (2) practitioners have an opportunity to reinforce their own standards as they appraise the practice of their colleagues; and (3) peer review dramatizes the truth that quality belongs to the practitioners, and not to management. The possibility of QA becoming a political football between union and management or between young professionals and their non-practising boss is greatly lessened by making peers the determiners of quality.

5.4. Management

Management has a role in the assessment of quality at two points. First, when quality assurance is beginning: at this stage, staff will need some orientation to, and even a role model in, quality assessment. The managers'/supervisors' intention is to work themselves out of a job. Second, where management sets the goals (a reduction in lost-time injuries, a more effective public education program, etc.): on these occasions, it must be management that decides whether its goals have been reached or surpassed.

5.5. Panels

There are some few occasions when the appraisal of a product or service can be performed more appropriately by people playing the role of consumer than professionals who are responsible for what is being reviewed. Taste-testing panels, readers of in-house publications, members of the public reviewing hospital outreach programs and materials would be some examples.

This concludes the review of the five steps in the planning of quality assessment.

6. Putting the Model to Work

If a department head were to use the Quality Assessment model, she would employ it in the *planning* of a review of her department's practice:

First, she would select a principal *function* as the topic for assessment. She would choose generally in the order of the function's importance.

Second, she would choose one or more aspects of the function as the subject(s) for assessment. She would recognize that the clearer the *focus*, the more likely she is to achieve clear answers. She would also see, from the list of foci, that the chosen function lacks available evidence on many aspects of its practice.

At Step III, the manager should involve the staff in the development or review of *standards and criteria* for the particular function. However, the

EXHIBIT 17

The Planning of Quality Assessment

FOCUS OF INQUIRY	EXPECTATIONS	METHOD OF INQUIRY	MAKING JUDGEMENTS
What to look *at?*	What to look *for?*	How to look?	Who determines Quality?
1. Goals or objectives	Standards & Criteria • Relevant • Understandable • Measurable • Behavioural • Achievable	1. Record the numbers	1. External agency

2. Structure & Resources
  2.1 People
  2.2 Equipment
  2.3 Environment
		2. Inspect the work
		3. Review charts and records
		4. Ask for opinions
			2. 0/1 answer
			3. Peers
			4. Management
			5. Panel

3. Methods & Procedures			

4. Outcome
  4.1 Productivity
  4.2 Quality of result
  4.3 Client satisfaction			

criteria list will not be finalized until she has determined how the selected function is going to be reviewed.

Step IV gives four options as to the *method of inquiry*, but the nature of the function and focus will probably make the determination.

The department head's final step is to choose and perhaps orient or train those who will carry out the assessment for the department.

After the assessment is completed, the data should be analyzed by the assessors and management; both should be involved in decisions as to remedial action, and in giving feed-back to staff. It is then the responsibility of the manager to report the study out of the department to her superior, and when the time is appropriate, to the hospital's QA Committee.

CHAPTER VII

Reporting and the QA Committee

In the early days of QA many administrators formed QA Committees and charged them with the responsibility of defining the meaning of *quality assurance* for the hospital and the roles that needed to be played in order that QA could be implemented successfully. Other hospitals relied on consultants to supply both definitions and start their programs. However they were started, today the leadership of QA programs is almost invariably in the hands of an in-house QA Committee. In this chapter we start with the Committee's Terms of Reference and then look at the Committee in action as it manages the program, leads the participants, evaluates submissions, and reports quality. Exhibit 18 lists twelve Terms of Reference for the QA Committee.

1. Terms of Reference

The QA Committee has two relationships: it acts for the Administrator; it works with department heads. For the CEO it provides "regular reports (Term 4)," "advice (7)," and "a procedure for program evaluation (12)." The Committee is carrying out a staff role in much the same way as does the Finance or Personnel departments. Both of these influence and account for, but do not control, the activities of line departments; so too does the QA Committee. Term 2 points to the fact that the Committee is not intended to have a permanent membership. Indeed, it is important that it does not. Instead, department heads and the assistant administrators should rotate off the committee after 18-24 months, so as to provide fresh ideas and energy. Crosby (1980, pp. 118-9; 221-2) is particularly good on this point. His Step 14 is, "Do it over again," and he deals with the rejuvenation of the QA team.

The QA Committee accomplishes its goals with the department heads through a process of influence. Its credibility depends initially on its

EXHIBIT 18

The Quality Assurance Committee

Terms of Reference

1. The Quality Assurance Committee is a management committee appointed by the Administrator to direct, monitor, and support the hospital's Quality Assurance Program.

2. The Committee shall report to the Administrator, who will appoint its members from time to time.

3. The Committee will be at all times conversant with the Accreditation Standards and the expectations of the Canadian Council on Hospital Accreditation.

4. The Committee is responsible for compiling regular reports for the Administrator to deliver to the Board and/or its standing committee according to a schedule determined by the Administrator.

5. The Committee is responsible for determining the steps to be taken by hospital departments in the development of a Quality Assurance Program, and the form in which they will report results and progress.

6. The Committee is responsible for providing encouragement and assistance to departments implementing QA programs. Such assistance may include the involvement of resource persons from inside and outside the hospital, the purchasing of books, journals, and audio-visual materials, and the sponsoring of management staff on QA conferences and seminars.

7. The Committee may make recommendations to the Administrator concerning changes in hospital policy and procedure which, in its view, are necessitated by considerations of Quality Assurance.

8. The Committee will report back to Department Heads on a quarterly basis, providing feedback on the development and results of the program.

9. The Committee is responsible for liaising with the Medical Staff and its QA endeavours.

10. The Committee is expected to observe "care or service" problems that occur *between* departments and to call on the parties involved to work together on problem-solving; their progress to be reported to the Committee.

11. The Committee will keep minutes and an inventory of resources used in the development of the hospital's program.

12. The Committee will develop, in consultation with the Administrator, a procedure under which the hospital's QA Program can be evaluated annually by the Board.

relationship with and mandate from the CEO. But this power of position is seldom, if ever, used. Instead, it gains respect by choosing the role of facilitator: "providing encouragement and assistance (6)," "calling on parties to work together (10)," and "providing feedback (8)." Respect also comes to the Committee as it demonstrates appropriate knowledge of QA (3) and makes correct and practical choices in its direction of the program (5). But there are two other significant features. First, the Committee never takes responsibility for anyone else's QA program. It will lead but not compel, advise but not prescribe. Second, its members exemplify what it is they are advising. The department heads on the committee are peers and colleagues of those whose compliance they need. They will do in their own departments what they are asking others to do in theirs. This requirement that Committee members exemplify what they expect of others has the additional merit of keeping the Committee's feet on the ground. It prevents useless exercises and inhibits the unreasonable escalation of demands on line managers.

2. The Committee in Action: Program Management

As program manager, the Committee's task is to decide where it wants to go and to find the easiest and quickest way to get there. In the early days of a QA program the QA Committee has to make a series of significant decisions and provisions:

- Choosing a QA model
- Deciding how to implement
- Identifying necessary internal and external resources
- Mapping the steps
- Designing the launch
- Finding/creating background material
- Creating general staff involvement
- Negotiating the Committee's own terms of reference
- Communicating with senior administration
- Setting assignments and dates

All of these items are program management.

The adult learning model owes many of its program components to QA Committees that have identified problems and fashioned solutions, tested the author's material and pronounced it practical or impossible. Let me give three examples, both as a demonstration of the management function of the Committees, and because the ideas are valuable in themselves.

2.1. Adapting ALM to Local Needs

When I wrote *Quality Assurance: Getting Started* in April 1985 we knew much more about the practicalities of the early stages of the model than the later ones. We had had good success with Stages I and II (Principal Functions and First Reports). Stage IV, the Introduction of Standards and Criteria, looked and has proved to be solid, but QA Planning and the Completion of Standards and Criteria for All Functions were still just ideas in a consultant's head. This is where QA Committees were of particular value. Their loyalty was not to any model but to the practicalities of their situation. They needed to have something that *worked* for their departments, and they forced me back to the drawing board more than once on QA Planning.

Once the format outlined (Ch. V.3) for QA Planning proved satisfactory, there was still the question of where it fitted best in the hospital's program. Some QA Committees insisted that their program go from Stage II (First Reports) to Stage IV (Introduction of Standards and Criteria), so as to enhance the quality of reporting early. On the other hand, some Committees recognized the value of early QA Planning (Stage III). Committees and department heads could become frustrated at not knowing where the program was going, or when it would arrive.

QA Committees have also acted helpfully when they experienced difficulty with Stage V: Standards and Criteria for All Principal Functions. The demands for this stage looked unreasonable in the short term or uncontrollable if done over a period of months. Fortunately, we experienced difficulty with this stage at a time when it was becoming obvious that accreditation surveyors were going to expect to see QA manuals, at least for the hospital as a whole, if not for each department. With two or three QA Committees at that time (January, 1986) we developed the process of Growing a Manual.

2.2. Growing a QA Manual

Hospitals and their departments need a convenient way of demonstrating that principal functions have been identified, an aspect of each has been assessed, and reports of these assessments have been forwarded up the line. Meanwhile, the QA Committee needs to demonstrate that the program it manages is coordinated, comprehensive, productive, and accountable. The vehicle for both was the QA manual.

For demonstration purposes and economy of effort it was clear that QA manuals should have a basic similarity. Accordingly, QA Committees have assumed the task is of choosing the uniform manual binder and developing the Contents page. Thereafter, departments were expected to drop into the manual in the appointed place items that corresponded to those listed by the Committee. It is this process of filling the Committee's prescription over a period of time that we call *growing* the manual. It takes shape gradually, and while the shape is fairly constant, the contents appropriate to each department vary widely from one to another.

The manual, when completed, should provide a full rationale for and access to all the resources used in the department's QA program. But the manual also carries a record of the department's continuous assessment of its principal functions. For this reason, the manual has two distinct parts: *QA Principles* and *QA Practice* (the QA Reports submitted to the QA Committee filed in chronological order).

Exhibit 19 is a sample Contents page developed for a 200-bed hospital. I have added a right-hand column which indicates the probable source of each document. From this column it is readily apparent that the development of the manual is not a task of writing or drafting, but one of retrieving and photocopying. Nor have we apologized for photocopying. Reliability in QA is more important than originality, and retrieval and integration of old standards is infinitely preferable to the creation of new.

QA manuals are intended to be tools and not ornaments put shining on the shelf and trotted out biennially or triennially for CCHA surveyors. They should be used and revised as better resources become available and when the department's own plan is in need of updating.

Exhibit 20 shows a sample Contents page for the QA Committee itself.

EXHIBIT 19

Departmental QA Manual: Contents Page

2.3. Scheduling Departmental Reports

In determining the frequency with which the various hospital departments should report their QA to the Committee, most QA Committees took the 1985 table (*Quality Assurance: Getting Started, Appendix N*) and modified it to suit their departments. But recently one hospital decided to do its own thinking. Its QA minutes describe how it solved the problem:

> [The QA Coordinator] suggested that a review of all departments be done to decide reporting frequency. . . . A discussion took place regarding the appropriateness and feasibility of monthly reporting. The Committee agreed that the following criteria would be used to determine frequency of reporting:

EXHIBIT 20

Hospital QA Manual: Contents Page

PART IA. The Hospital-wide Program

1.	QA Policy Statement	Board
2.	CCHA QA Standards	1985 pp. 45–47
3	Organizational Chart of Hospital-wide Program	Figure 1
4.	Terms of Reference of Board QA Committee	Exhibit 18
5.	Liaison Activities with MAC and/or Medical Audit and Tissue Committee	
6.	Terms of Reference of Hospital-wide Committees:	
	6.1 Occupational Health and Safety	Administration
	6.2 Fire and Disaster	Administration
	6.3 Infection Control	Administration
7.	List of External Bodies Authorized to Inspect Hospital/Departments, with Frequency	Administration
8.	Report of Last CCHA Survey	Administration

PART IB. QA Program Led by QA Committee

9.	Frequency of Departmental Reporting to QA Committee	Exhibit 21
10.	Policy Statements/Educational Programs Designed by QA Committee	Committee
11.	QA Forms Authorized by Committee	Committee

PART II Monthly QA Reports

QA Reports submitted monthly to CEO, filed chronologically

Figure/Exhibit numbers refer to this book.

1. intimacy of clinical relationship with patient (impact on patient care).

2. need of department for experience in reporting.

3. size of department.

4. focus of Accreditation surveyors—Nursing, Environmental Safety (Safety, Occupational Health, Housekeeping, Engineering), Emergency and Pharmacy.

It was agreed that, based on scoring, reporting would be done as follows: 4/4 monthly, 3/4 bi-monthly, 2/4 quarterly and 1/4 semi-annually. A review of each department was done, results of which are detailed on the attached chart [Exhibit 21].

EXHIBIT 21

Hospital Departments: Criteria for Reporting Frequency

DEPARTMENT	PATIENT IMPACT	PRACTICE	SIZE	ACCREDI-TATION	TOTAL	REPORTING FREQUENCY
Accounting		X			1	semiannual
Admitting	X	X			2	quarterly
Business Office	X		X		2	quarterly
CSR		X	X		2	semiannual
Chaplaincy	X	X			2	quarterly
Chiropody	X	X			2	semiannual
Day Nursery		X			1	semiannual
Engineering		X	X	X	3	bimonthly
Food Services	X		X		2	quarterly
Housekeeping	X	X	X	X	4	bimonthly
Infection Control	X			X	2	quarterly
Laboratory	X		X		2	quarterly
Medical Records	X				1	semiannual
Nursing	X	X	X	X	4	monthly
Occupational Health				X	1	semiannual
Payroll		X			1	semiannual
Personnel		X			1	semiannual
Pharmacy	X		X	X	3	bimonthly
Physical Medicine	X		X		2	quarterly
Purchasing		X			1	semiannual
Radiology	X				1	semiannual
Safety	X	X		X	3	bimonthly
Social Work	X		X		2	quarterly
Staff Development					0	semiannual
Stores		X			1	semiannual
Switchboard	X	X			2	semiannual
Volunteer Services	X				1	semiannual

3. Leadership

For some people, QA programs mean bureaucracy and a surfeit of paper, or a plethora of measurements and statistics. For me QA is a "people program." Its most important messages concern people (patients); they are generated by people (front line workers) and are considered, acted upon and transmitted by at least three echelons of people (department heads, the QA Committee, Administration and the Board). Because QA programs are people programs they have the potential to be enjoyable and to be the source of personal and professional satisfaction. We see this in the programs whose implementation we direct, and we value highly those emphasis weeks which Committees organize to keep alive the value and enjoyment in the quest for quality.

Leadership is both setting the right course—the topic of the last section, Program Management—and helping people to follow it, which is our present topic. We decided early that the Committee could lead best if individual members took responsibility for coaching a limited number of compatible departments. If this could be done successfully, it would cut down on the number of memos going out from the Committee and make its requirements more personal and acceptable to those affected.

3.1. Liaison

Nothing epitomizes better the people aspect of QA and leadership through influence than the liaison task assigned to all QA Committee members. What is now an integral part of the adult learning model came about through the admission of ignorance with which many QA Committees began their work. In essence they said, "We don't know what exactly we are looking for (in Principal Functions or First QA Reports), so we will all give it our best shot and then criticize our own efforts, before we criticize those of others. When we have made up our minds as a committee, each of us will sit down with the other department heads and tell them, one-on-one, what looks good and how we did it in our own situations." Thus, liaison provides an organized communications network through which the Committee can coach, test, criticize and reinforce. It has suited the needs of those starting QA programs in that Committee members were quite unwilling and unprepared to act as "experts." Other department heads have found QA easier to handle as a group exploration rather than as conformity to the demands of experts.

At later stages in the life of QA programs, it is expected that liaison will make it easier for other department heads to join the Committee as new members. It may be important to retain this liaison aspect of Committee function when QA reporting becomes more complicated and carries more data. Liaison keeps ownership of the process low in the organization and ensures that leadership is a function that is exercised by peers. Figures 9 and 10 show different principles on which Committee liaison can be organized. Figure 9 shows the QA Committee communicating with organized structures: Hospital Services, Nursing, etc. This model best fits larger hospitals where all the clinical and support departments are organized into separate divisions, each reporting to an Assistant Administrator or Vice-president. Often these divisions will organize their own divisional QA Committee, in the same way that nursing departments (always the largest of the divisions) have their own QA or Audit Committees. Figure 10 shows an *ad hoc* model used in smaller hospitals where other considerations are more important. Among these might be geography, similarity of function, the need to pair the experienced with those needing more help, and so on.

3.2. Leadership and Common Problems

Most QA Committees, at one time or another, have to cope with certain problems. Four are identified and their treatment discussed in the next sections.

3.2.1 The Unable.   Department heads in a hospital have a wide variety of educational backgrounds and management experience. In QA some are found

FIGURE 9

Liaison through Representatives: QA Committee in a Large Hospital

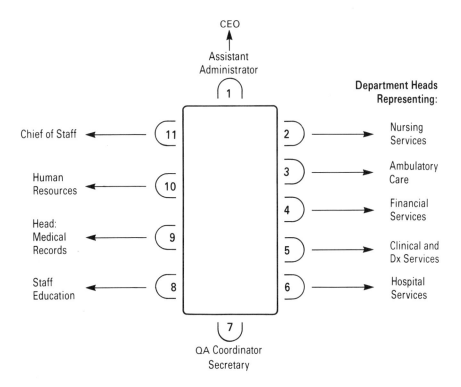

to be half-way down the track before the starter's gun has been fired—typically, the managers of Laboratories, Radiology and Physiotherapy. Others just seem to stand bewildered and startled when they hear the shot. The task of the QA Committee is to get all the runners on the track heading in the same direction, at about the same speed.

Supervisors of housekeeping, food services, engineering and maintenance in small hospitals are often discouraged by QA. They are "hands-on people" and shy of paper work. They are also sensitive about being made to look foolish in front of their supervisors or managers. All will have a QA Committee member assigned to work with them, whose task it will be to show them (1) that they are already doing QA, although they do not call it that; (2) that the program tasks are simple and practical; (3) that QA assessment begins with the assessing or monitoring they are already doing; and (4) that peer help is readily available. Is this familiar? It should be, as these are the basic truths that ALM uses to get everyone on side and active.

3.2.2 The Unwilling. Then there are those who would love to perform QA, but feel it cannot be done in their departments; there seems nothing tangible to

FIGURE 10

Organized Liaison of a QA Committee in a Small Hospital

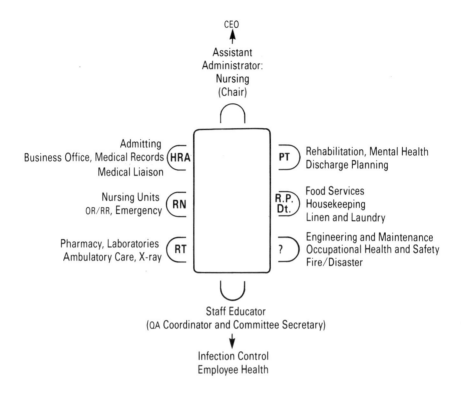

manage, and besides they don't have time, and patient care comes first. The correct strategy here is often to provide lots of understanding and leave them alone. It is important, neither to endorse their views of the impossibility of QA, nor to offer help or advice before they ask for it. In nine cases out of ten the unwilling will come around when they find that less-qualified managers are doing QA without apparent difficulty. The threat of future embarrassment before their boss or their peers is usually a powerful incentive. The QA Committee neither gets into fights with its clients nor tells tales out of school by letting the CEO know about the non-compliant.

3.2.3 The Embarrassers. I remember one Nursing Coordinator complaining at the QA Committee meeting that she was tired of seeing Nursing scapegoated in everyone else's QA reports. Somehow her department was getting blamed for matters she had never heard raised as problems before. What stance was the Committee to take? My advice was very direct: (1) that the Committee should not consider any report that made allegations against another

department unless the reporting department could show that it had attempted to resolve the issue; and (2) that the liaison person was responsible for keeping off the Committee's table one-sided or tale-carrying reports.

3.2.4 The Inhibitors.   On the other hand, in such a complex organization as a hospital some aspects of care and service are neglected because they fall between two stools. Equally often, the quality of one department's service will be endangered by the failure of another department to perform an essential service for the first. Departments frequently have quite different priorities: service from your department may be essential to me, but of secondary importance to you. QA Committees will recognize these common situations and must address them when they occur for the sake of the patient, and for the sake of the hospital. The Committee will insist on consultation (3.2.3 above), will ignore political arguments (those based on the size or prestige of the non-performing department/individual), and will call for joint discussions, and/or parallel studies (i.e., of same problem) by both departments. The Committee would expect to be informed of the departments' results—their problem resolution or the conclusions of their study.

4. QA Reporting

QA reports are the essential communications medium of the QA Committee. Through them it monitors the health of departmental programs; Committee feedback to departments is based upon their efforts demonstrated in QA reports. The QA Committee communicates to the CEO and beyond him or her to the board by means of monthly reports. Outlined in this section are some expectations as to content and frequency, along with a discussion of two different types of reports, and suggest some guidelines for the monthly reports rendered by the QA Committee to the CEO.

4.1. Frequency

There is an important distinction between the frequency with which individual departments render reports to the QA Committee and the regularity with which they should assess their performance. The QA Committee's determination of reporting frequency is part of its own stewardship of time. It is based on the Committee's realization that it cannot review reports from every department every month and give them the scrutiny they deserve. Accordingly, it spreads the load over a six-month period, as outlined above (Section 2.3). But when it establishes its schedule the QA Committee establishes its general rule: *all departments will evaluate an aspect of their work every month*. The fact that the QA Committee does not need to hear from Housekeeping each month does not affect the department's need to monitor its performance with the same regularity as any other.

No department or nursing unit reports to the QA Committee more frequently than every second month. At the time of their reporting they may (1) present all their reports compiled since their last appearance, or (2) present one of their choosing and summarize other studies completed in the interim. They have access to the committee through their liaison member. At the same time the QA Committee can ask for more frequent reports if it becomes concerned about a slippage in standards.

4.2. Content

QA reports will generally deal with aspects of performance assessment, the fourth of our QA components. There may be times when goals/standards or quality promotion activities are significant enough to be the topic of a report, but this will be unusual. Generally speaking, routine activity monitoring, while important, will merit special reporting only when its systems fail or change. The reports that will call for the Committee's particular attention will be quality reviews (analyses of existing data), quality evaluation (audits and special studies) and quality approval (outside and client assessments of the department's service).

4.3. Quality Assessment Reports

QA reporting forms are like performance appraisal forms. No matter what you start with, you will want to change them within three months. We should, however, note the tendency to make the form more demanding and specific, and its completion more mechanical. This makes sense if the information is to be abstracted and logged, whether manually or by computer. But if the QA report is intended to give a one-time summary and message, then we need to reverse the trend and make the report simpler, and its message more direct. Above, we have described a QA report as

> one that states what you examined, how you examined it, what you found, how that was significant, and what you did or intended to do about it.

4.4. Reports of Leading Indicators

Increasingly, department heads will be expected to render monthly reports on performance indicators that are descriptive of the general quality of their departments. These can be positive and/or negative, expressing the attainment of quality standards and/or the breach of a zero standard (i.e., the occurrence of something that should never happen). The following paragraph from the minutes of a QA Committee reveals this mixture:

> *Laboratory*
> Audits were received for the months of November and December 1985, and January 1986.
> *November 1985—Internal* Quality Control was satisfactory with problems of Quality Control of one chemistry analyser which was reported to Administration. *External* Quality Control (LPTP) was unsatisfactory due to reporting error made in enzyme chemistry. *Safety* was satisfactory and there were 2 minor needle-prick injuries which required hepatitis immunization. One *staff evaluation* was unsatisfactory which will be re-

EXHIBIT 22

Quality Assurance Report (1986)	
A. Department and Section	
B. Date of Report	C. Period of Assessment
I What did you look at? (FOCUS)	
II How did you look? (MEANS)	
III What did you find? (FINDINGS)	
IV How was that SIGNIFICANT?	
V What are you going to do about III? (FOLLOW-UP)	
Response of QA Committee:	

evaluated in three months. *Equipment maintenance* audit showed a knife sharpener could not be repaired due to being outdated and no parts available and has been budgeted for 1986. [Emphasis added.]

From the December and January summaries, it is clear that this department is compiling monthly data on five variables: Internal QC, External QC (i.e., LPTP), Safety, Equipment Maintenance, and Staff performance appraisal. These data are reported to the QA Committee quarterly.

4.5. The CEO's QA Report

The QA Committee may be responsible for reporting QA not only to the CEO, but in so doing for providing the essential text that the CEO will take to the Board or Board QA Committee. This is the meaning of the fourth of its Terms of Reference (Exhibit 18). Thus it behooves both the Administrator and the QA Committee to consider what information trustees will find intelligible and significant. In general, we should expect hospital boards to value most highly evidence of the hospital's performance obtained from outside and information related to the hospital's liability. Trustees are likely to show a marked preference for clinical achievement over administrative or support services data, and be interested in hospital-wide programs over those of individual departments. While individual boards will rank their priorities differently, the following five classes of data are likely to be on their list, probably much as in the order given:

4.5.1 External Reviews.
Boards will instinctively prefer reports of assessments of the hospital's performance from outsiders to data gathered by staff. The outsider's information is independent, and expert because the agency reviews many such institutions.

4.5.2 Risk Management.
All information that indicates the hospital, its employees or patients are or have been at risk should be reported. Obvious indications of risk include: suits or complaints against the hospital, employee grievances, patient incidents, lost-time injuries, inquests and inquiries. These should be reported to the board in a manner and frequency appropriate to each.

4.5.3 Client Satisfaction.
Although we realize that information from patients may not be clinically reliable, it does and should carry weight with senior management and the board. Patients are sensitive to the human and interpersonal values and performance of the hospital. The way in which care is given is an integral part of the care itself. The trustees representing the community want to know what people like themselves think of the hospital's caring.

4.5.4 Hospital-wide Programs.
Over the years, several quality control/risk management issues have been organized on a hospital-wide basis. The most prominent of these in Ontario are Occupational Health and Safety, Fire and Disaster Preparedness, and Infection Control. There may be merit also in treating the personnel function as a hospital-wide program since its elements

Credibility of QA Data from the Viewpoint of the Trustee

QA COMPONENTS	TRUSTEES' PRIORITIES IN QA
1.1 Goal Setting	
1.2 Standard Setting	
2. Q Promotion	
3.1 Q Control	
3.2 Q Supervision	#2 Incidents/Occurrences
4.1 Q Review	#4 Hospital-wide Programs
4.2 Q Evaluation	#5 Clinical Audits
4.3 Q Approval	
External agencies	#1 External Reviews
Patients	#3 Client Satisfaction
In-house clients	

and administration are shared by every department: recruitment, orientation, appraisal, employee relations, and staff development.

4.5.5 Quality Assessment.   Boards will be interested in both the hospital's attempt to measure its performance and in the results of such evaluations. Initially, they will be more assured by the fact that reviews are being undertaken than by what is discovered. This will change as they become more expert and can readily understand the data and discuss their significance. Trustees, sensibly, will be most concerned with data that reflect on patients and their care and safety. Service departments have to live with this priority, as a fact of life.

5. Evaluation

In this section I have reproduced, verbatim, four QA reports presented to one QA Committee and have noted the Committee's response to each in a concluding paragraph. Two other Committee interactions are taken from other hospitals to provide additional examples of the *evaluation* function of the QA Committee.

5.1. Purchasing and Stores

Function Assessed: Inventory Control—regular issuing of materials from inventory.

Focus: Supply and distribution of printed material for all departments.

Method of Inquiry: Discussion with department employee to determine quantity of printed material.

Principal Findings:
1. Supply and distribution of printed material is now shared with the Business Office.
2. No master list exists to determine the true quantity of currently used forms, and those which are now defunct.
3. There are no hospital-wide standards used in the production of new printed material.
4. Increased demand for printed material has resulted in increased work load.

Recommendations:
1. A master list be produced of all hospital printed material in use, and the need for each reviewed with users.
2. Standards be set to facilitate production of new forms.

Committee Response: It was clear from the findings that the department was asking questions of a completely unregulated function. The Committee recommended clarification of responsibility for forms control: *either* the Business Office *or* Purchasing should be responsible. It endorsed the recommended actions and hoped their implementation would allow a more controlled study at the next reassessment date.

5.2. Dietary

Function Assessed:
1. Providing nutrition consultation and education services.
2. Maintaining the department at an optimum sanitary level.

Focus: Education in Food Safety in Health Care Institutions.

Method of Inquiry: An educational program was received from the Ontario Ministry of Health consisting of six video presentations and accompanying quizzes.

Principal Findings:
1. Seven of the eleven Dietary Department employees have completed the program and received their certificates.
2. Four members still have to complete the course.
3. The program was ideal for the department because it was directed specifically at food handlers in health care institutions. It was thorough in that it discussed all aspects of sanitation in food services and followed through in asking questions on the material presented.

Intended Actions and Recommendations:
Action:
1. The four staff members will complete the program by Wednesday, April 9, 1986.
2. All quizzes will be given every six months.

Recommendations:
This program will be used to orientate new employees.

Proposed Reassessment Date: September, 1986.

Committee Response: The Committee rightly saw this report as dealing with Quality Investment in the competence of staff. It endorsed Function 2 as the more appropriate, and approved the Recommendation and the Reassessment date.

5.3. Medical Records

Function Assessed: Quantitative Analysis of in-patient and out-patient records.

Focus: The Quantitative Analysis of in-patient records.

Method of Inquiry: Ten charts were picked at random from a list of January, 1986, discharged patients. Each chart was evaluated for its content by the criteria on the Monthly Review Worksheet. The criteria on the worksheet were compiled according to departmental policies and accreditation standards for patient records and their content.

Principal Findings:
1. On admission histories dictated, three out of ten lacked documentation in regard to past illness; six out of ten made no mention of family history.
2. Four out of ten charts reviewed lacked progress notes, but in three the LOS [length of stay] was less than three days, in which case a final note is considered sufficient. One chart had an LOS of seven days which, according to Accreditation Standards, warrants more documentation.
3. Out of the ten Discharge Summaries that were reviewed, seven made no mention of Admitting or Final Diagnosis; three out of ten lacked documentation on the patient's condition on discharge. This was felt to be a critical area for improvement, as it was one of the recommendations by hospital accreditation.
4. On seven out of ten charts, nursing signatures were required in *one* of the following areas: Graphics, Medication Sheets and Nurses' Notes.

Intended Actions and Recommendations:
1. Closer scrutiny of charts by medical records personnel when completing daily deficiency slips (Quantitative Analysis).
2. Reacquaint the physicians with items that should be contained in Admission Histories and Discharge Summaries when they are dictated.

Recommendations:
Recommend the results of monthly chart reviews be given to Medical Records Committee so that the Physicians and Nursing Department are informed of the deficiencies in these areas.

Proposed Reassessment Date: This will be a monthly review—April 1986.

Committee Response: While the sample size was small, the Committee viewed the study as worthwhile and its findings highly significant. Both Medical

Records and the contributors to the charts (MDs and RNs) were shown to be deficient. It endorsed both the recommendation and making this review a *monthly* assessment.

5.4. Business Office

Function Assessed: Processing all documentation related to all in-patients and out-patients, including admissions and discharges.

Focus: Assessing compatibility of patient ID cards with present admitting report form.

Method of Inquiry: Discussion with those employees responsible for completing admitting report form.

Principal Findings: Admission information using an ID card is more accurate.

Committee Response: While the Committee had no quarrel with the usefulness of the study it had major problems with the means employed. It reasoned that a straight comparison of the error rates of the two forms concerned would be much more reliable than a discussion of their use. The latter may usefully occur after the findings have been developed.

Two further examples come from other hospitals.

5.5. Housekeeping

The Housekeeping Department recently began evaluating the performance of its cleaners and maids. By documenting the results on special Housekeeping "Inspection List" forms, the necessary information allows us to monitor levels of cleanliness throughout the hospital and to improve levels where necessary.

Supervisors inspect "cleaned" areas on a regular basis using these forms. They decide, on a four-level scale from "poor" to "excellent," the cleanliness of floors, corners and baseboards, drapes, walls, bathrooms, carpets, stairs, elevators, and equipment for cleaners. Maids are evaluated on the cleanliness of such items as sinks, beds, garbage cans, furniture, bathrooms, corridors, fridges, hoppers and their own carts.

The Supervisor discusses findings of the inspection directly with the employee. Problem areas are reviewed and corrective suggestions are made. After a reasonable length of time for improvement to be shown, a second inspection occurs. If insufficient improvement is shown then the cleaning technique is reviewed or special training and job review is given. If this does not produce the desired change, then an appointment may be made for the employee to discuss his/her performance with the Executive Housekeeper.

Committee Response: While it found the study to be useful and valid, the Committee noted the department's confusion of QA with performance appraisal (PA), and was very concerned at the threat implied in the last sentence. The liaison member was deputized to explain the fundamental difference between QA and PA and recommend that (1) housekeeping staff should play a part in the appraising and (2) that rooms should be appraised and not people. The minutes read: "It was felt that the problem [of poor cleaning] was not non-compliance, but rather the use of the wrong process, equipment, etc. The action should perhaps be an in-service, a change in system or the environment, not discipline."

5.6. Nursing: Patient Safety

The nursing procedure required staff to check the ward emergency equipment and supplies on each shift and endorse the sign-off sheet to signify that the check had been done. A total of 76 sign-off sheets were reviewed over a five-month period by the Audit Committee. Of these, 50 percent indicated that the above standard was *not* being met. Deviations ranged from missing one check per week to missing several. However, the Audit Committee satisfied itself that in all cases, at the time of the audit, the emergency equipment was complete and in working order. It offered five alternative explanations of the department's lack of compliance. Nursing intention and corrective action was to reinforce the standard and look for early compliance.

Committee Response: The hospital QA Committee was not convinced that this was the right course, and requested a re-evaluation of the standard. It wondered whether the procedure had lost its meaning to staff by its frequent repetition and the invariable finding that all was complete and correct.

These six examples show how QA Committees can respond appropriately to departments on the basis of their reports. They can confirm (Dietary) or dissent (Nursing), endorse and encourage (Medical Records), re-educate (Housekeeping) and advise on audit methods (Business Office) and intended actions (ditto). They will also be concerned with the intelligibility of the reports to the layman, and that the conclusions (findings) are appropriate to the data submitted.

Through the evaluation of QA reports reaching it the QA Committee will monitor, and by its responses raise the quality of the hospital's QA program. It is looking for significant investigations carried out in appropriate ways, whose stated findings match the data presented. It wants to see remedial action and recommendations that address the deficiencies discovered and a re-audit frequency that matches significance of the findings.

6. A Thousand Words

The Lab Manager gave the author a tour, explaining her QA and quality control program while going from lab to lab, from Chemistry to Bacteriology and so on. At each lab there was a bulletin board on which was a set of flow sheets, one for each QC procedure to be carried out routinely. They had plotted a band of acceptable values (between 0.4 and 0.7 or 2,500 to 3,000) on the graph and daily recorded the latest reading, linking it with the actual for the preceding day. They showed the labs' achievement of acceptable results nineteen times out of twenty. After a while, the graphs appeared tedious, except that anyone could see at a glance that staff and equipment were up to snuff. Then we came to a graph that showed the lab's values to be quite erratic.

"What is going on here?".

"These are the White Count values," the lab manager replied. "We are having trouble with their linearity. You can see the values are within the acceptable band, but the low control is consistently running high and the high control is consistently running low. We think it is the analyzer. We've had the company in to look at it." And she pointed to some check marks to show when the supplier had made adjustments. "But they don't seem to be able to track down the problem. It is a 15-year-old machine. We are just going to have to retire it."

And they did. Using the QC charts and equipment records, she was able to show the Administrator what the problem was and how they had tried, without success, to correct it. This documentation helped the board to make a $150,000 decision promptly and with well-informed confidence.

If communicating quality is next in importance to its delivery in patient care service, then QA Committees must press for the early use of data illustration. It gets the message across quickly and powerfully, and the three basic pictures are easy to use. We are referring to the *pie chart*, the *bar graph*, and the *line diagram*.

6.1. The Pie Chart

The pie chart is excellent for the portrayal of percentages, where the pie represents 100 percent and the various slices different percentages. A department could use a pie chart to illustrate the comparative time/cost of carrying out its various principal functions. The attribution of medical-surgical supply costs to the hospital's six units/cost centres could also be portrayed on a pie chart. Pie charts have limitations. They will not carry serial data (this month versus last month) unless you use two pies side by side or employ some fancy shading. Nor will they carry unrelated data (the percentage of those on special diets who were satisfied with the food compared with the percentage of those on general menu who were satisfied). Figure 11 uses two pie charts to make a comparison between the size of nursing services and their consumption of total nursing budget.

6.2. The Bar Graph

The bar graph or histogram can be used to show quantities (by the height of each column) of any number of individual variables. We could use a bar graph to show the number (or percentage) of staff in each department who were qualified in CPR. Or the different columns could represent not departments but serial dates: the number of delinquent charts at 30 days, this

FIGURE 11

The Pie Chart: Clinical Services by Beds and by Allocation of Nursing Budget

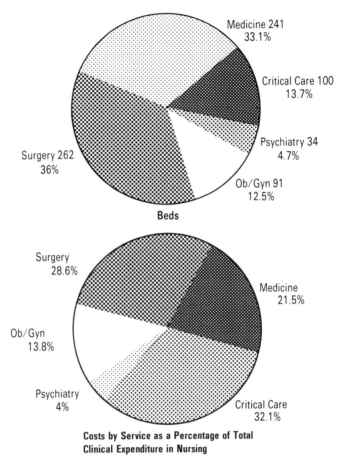

Medicine 241
33.1%

Critical Care 100
13.7%

Psychiatry 34
4.7%

Ob/Gyn 91
12.5%

Surgery 262
36%

Beds

Surgery
28.6%

Medicine
21.5%

Ob/Gyn
13.8%

Psychiatry
4%

Critical Care
32.1%

**Costs by Service as a Percentage of Total
Clinical Expenditure in Nursing**

month *versus* last month and so on. Columns can show one total—the height of the column, or by shading, two or more subtotals in addition. Figure 12 shows the volume of different categories of patients presenting to the admitting department by time of day.

6.3. The Line Diagram

The line diagram represents a series of measurements of the same variable, such as fuel consumption per week over the year. This series of totals could be compared easily with a second line plotted on the same graph (e.g., average weekly temperatures at noon) to give an idea of fuel efficiency. The scales would be carried on the *left* in hundreds of cubic metres/litres of fuel, and on the *right* as the noon temperature in degrees Celsius. In Figure 13 a comparison is shown between a hospital's frequency of lost-time accidents by month in three successive years.

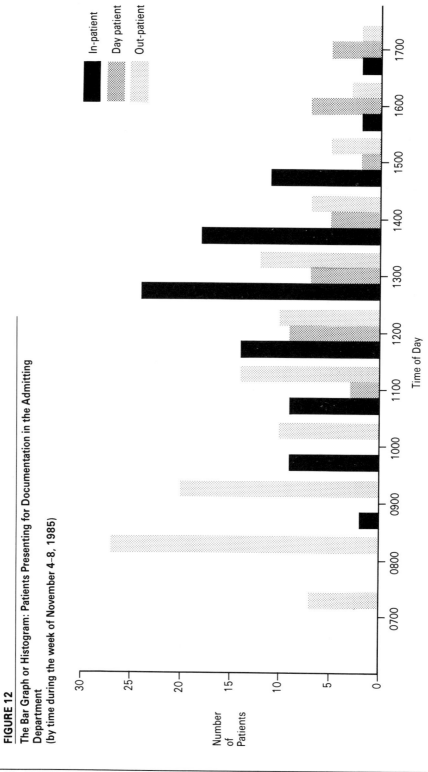

FIGURE 12

The Bar Graph or Histogram: Patients Presenting for Documentation in the Admitting Department
(by time during the week of November 4–8, 1985)

FIGURE 13

The Line Diagram: Occurrence of Lost-time Accidents
in an Acute Public General Hospital
by Month of First Payment of Claim

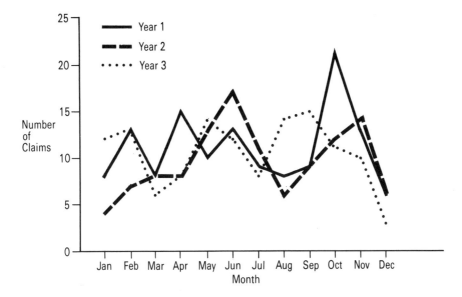

The QA Committee can encourage departments to use illustrations, by providing blanks, by letting them know that a free-hand diagram is acceptable, and by sponsoring an invitational workshop on "Communicating Results: Statistics and Illustration" for its members and those heading departmental programs.

CHAPTER VIII

Quality Assurance and the Hospital Board

1. The Role Assigned

Trustees have been conspicuously neglected in the last five chapters, in which were detailed the organization and implementation of the Quality Assurance program within the hospital. This neglect could imply that Boards of Trustees have only a subsidiary role to play in QA. But the truth is quite the contrary. The quality assurance loop which begins with the care given to the *patient* is completed only when the lay member of the community, the trustee, assures his and the *patient's community* that the care delivered in its hospital is safe, reliable, and excellent. Second, in the public hospital where hospital and medical staff report independently to the Board, it is only at trustee level that both sides of the QA program come together. Third, QA is the major program through which the hospital can render account to its governors concerning its essential mission: patient care. It is quite appropriate to say that, as well as having intrinsic merit at every level at which it is practised, QA is ultimately trustee assurance or public assurance. This is an important matter in today's open society.

This chapter, which incorporates some of the material reviewed in Chapter II, Section 7, is written particularly for trustee readers. They may question why professionals are addressed in five chapters and they in one only! One day they should have a whole book addressed to their role as governors of the clinical affairs of the hospital. In the meantime, it is intended that this chapter should outline the duties expected of boards by the Canadian Council on Hospital Accreditation and provide practical strategies to fulfill them.

According to the 1985 *Standards*, hospital governing bodies have four responsibilities in respect of QA:

1. For the effectiveness and comprehensiveness of the hospital-wide program,

   an institution-wide quality assurance program is an essential element for accreditation. This program must include review and evaluation of medical, nursing and other direct patient care departments and also evaluation of the delivery of support services as well as performance appraisal of personnel. The governing body shall be responsible for and shall provide the necessary resources to carry this out (Governing Body and Administration Standard VII, p. 13).

2. For examining the reports of the QA program:

   Through individual and/or committee reporting, the chief executive officer ensures that the governing body receives regular reports on and results of all aspects of the quality assurance program. Actions taken as a consequence of the program are also reported to ensure that the governing body fulfills its mandate in ensuring and being accountable for the delivery of optimal quality care (*ibid.*).

3. For examining the reports of the Utilization Review program:

   There shall be appropriate review methods and procedures in place to ensure that patient care resources are utilized effectively and efficiently and that potentials for improvement are diligently pursued.

   It is essential that the observations, comments and recommendations of the Utilization Review Committee be reported to the institution's governing body. This should be accompanied, of course, with any additional information or recommendations the Medical Advisory Committee, or equivalent, may wish to add (*ibid.*, Utilization Review).

4. For evaluating its own function as a board:

   The Board shall develop a methodology of evaluating its own function and the governance of the health care facility. Methodologies may include a structured self-evaluating program or the use of outside resources to effect a periodic strategic review of the mission and functions of the health care facility (*ibid.*, Review of Governance).

2. The Organization of the QA Program

The Board, having the overall responsibility for the conduct of the health care facility, shall initiate and support the development of a facility-wide quality assurance program to assure the attainment of the goals of the health care facility in support of the board-approved mission statement.

The development and coordination of the quality assurance program may be accomplished through a committee, group or individual. The organizational structure shall be determined by the Board on the advice of the administration and the professional and other staffs of the health care facility (*Standards*, p. 46).

The *Standards* lay the responsibility of the QA program squarely at the door of the board of trustees. In spite of the fact that in-house organization and program development are generally considered to be the responsibility of senior management the *Standards* uses terms such as "initiate and support," "determine organizational structure" and "provide resources" to delineate the *Board's* role. Clearly, the Council wishes to see that Boards have a sense of ownership of these programs.

The previous chapters have outlined how a QA program can be started and organized, and have specified roles that should be played by staff at various levels in the hospital. In this section we look at a second organizational structure and discuss how the Board organizes itself to carry out its role in the total QA program.

2.1. Organizational Structure

Chapter II recommended that the QA program should be organized around the bi-modal organizational structure in which administration and medical staff report in parallel separately to the Board. But how about those hospitals that are organized on the European pattern, with one Chief Executive Officer to whom all financial, support, professional and medical services report? The same advice holds: follow the existing organizational structure.

In Canada, psychiatric hospitals owned and operated by provincial governments are the most common examples of the uni-modal health care organization. In these hospitals, the physicians and psychiatrists, through the Medical Advisory Committee, report to Administration as do all the usual departments: nursing and the paramedical departments, finance and support services. The chair of the MAC is held by the salaried Chief of Staff, who is often called Medical Director. He or she may also be the same person that chairs the Professional Advisory Committee, which oversees the multidisciplinary clinical programs. Figure 14 may help to simplify a complex structure in which there are three hierarchies: Nursing, Hospital (i.e., finance and support) Services, and Professional Services, and two advisory committees: MAC (medical staff) and the Professional Advisory Committee, PAC (multidisciplinary programs).

These advisory bodies can best be used if each of them forms a QA Committee to undertake and/or to manage QA for those reporting to it. The role of each of these QA Committees is analogous to those of the QA Coordinating Committee and the MAC in the bi-modal organization. In turn each will report QA to a hospital-wide QA Committee (in the centre of the diagram), which will act in many respects like the QA Committee of the Board, in governing the whole program for and with the CEO.

2.2. The QA Committee of the Board

Because of the importance and complexity of the hospital's finances, Boards usually delegate their surveillance to a committee. In most Board organizations, the Finance Committee is the most active and principal standing

FIGURE 14

Organization of the QA Program in a Psychiatric Hospital

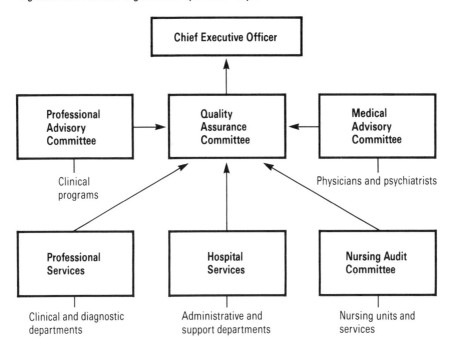

committee. These committees meet before each regular meeting of the Board and receive and scrutinize the hospital's accounts for the preceding month(s). Often the Treasurer will go over the accounts in detail with the hospital's Director of Finance, so that he or she can lead his or her own committee's scrutiny and present the accounts to the full Board, with the committee's endorsement. The committee will also be responsible for the consideration of the hospital's annual budget submissions, and the reception of the annual report from the hospital's auditor. We recommend the Board's establishment of a Quality Assurance Committee in a direct parallel with the Finance Committee, for the same reasons, meeting with the same frequency, and discharging the same responsibility for the hospital's accounts of care. It should take responsibility for the hospital's QA plan (budget), and consider the reports of outside examiners on the hospital's care and services.

Given below are terms of reference developed by the Ontario Hospital Association for QA Committees of the Board. As the preamble (Exhibit 24) states, some Boards may choose the alternative of using an existing committee in preference to establishing a new one. Many hospital Boards already have a committee with some patient care mandate. When consulting, we have recommended that the Board can enlarge the Committee's existing terms of reference to include the full QA responsibility. Not a few Boards have felt that they already have too many committees. In these circumstances, they can breathe new life into one of them by giving the Committee responsibility for

QA. This latter strategy has worked particularly well in respect of Joint Conference Committees (JCC). In Ontario JCCs are usually standing committees of the Board. They are composed of the chairman and two lay members of the Board, three members of the medical staff, and the administrator. They are designed to resolve Administration-medical staff and medical staff-Board problems, but it is not unusual to find that they lack an agenda from year to year and fail to hold the number of meetings prescribed in the hospital by-laws. Their Board, medical staff and Administration composition has seemed, to many hospitals, tailor-made for QA.

If a Board chooses to establish a new Committee, then, as will be seen from the proposed terms of reference, it should have a majority of lay trustees, one of whom should be in the chair. It is worth keeping the Committee small and maintaining good continuity in its membership, so that trustees can have the opportunity of developing the desired competence.

The recommendation that QA should be reported first to a committee of the Board has not been universally accepted. We should look at two alternatives recommended by hospitals. Some hospitals insist that Quality Assurance reports be made to the full Board, such is their importance. The logic in this reporting is faulty. If, as we believe, QA reports are so important, they should be considered by a hand-picked committee, with the opportunity for questions and dialogue. Ten minutes at a full Board meeting is an indignity to the Board and the topic of quality of care. Let the reports be studied and let the Committee advise the Board. If the hospital is that convinced of the importance of QA, then it should have QA reported to the Management or Executive Committee of the Board. That should satisfy everyone.

Many hospitals are involving trustees at much earlier stages in the QA chain. Not a few have them serve as members of the hospital's QA Committee. Some even have one or two sitting on the Medical Audit Committee. How do these structures work? As far as one can tell, they seem a great success, the trustees learn a lot, and the hospitals swear by them. Would I endorse their use by others? In no way! One of the essential characteristics of trustees is their independence. To me putting the trustee on the hospital committee seems not unlike putting the auditor on the company payroll or indoctrinating the government inspector. And what will the Administrator say when some of the trustees start supporting physicians or hospital staff on the Committee against some of the Administrator's policies and decisions? He or she will want to blow the whistle, call "interference," and ask the Board President to speak to the offender(s). But who put the trustee on the in-house Committee in the first place and asked him or her to get involved?

Active QA programs should report regularly to a sharp and *independent* committee of the Board. The troops going on parade would be quite slovenly were it not for the sergeant's inspection; the sergeant's review would be quite cursory were it not for the subaltern's inspection; and the subaltern might hurry through it, if he or she were not expecting the company commander. QA leaders need the stimulus of having to strut their stuff before an acute audience which then has to make their data its own before the full Board.

2.3. Terms of Reference

The terms of reference included below are five in number. They indicate first that both hospital and medical staff QA be reported to the same Board committee, on a monthly basis. While there should be no problem with the hospital's reporting, we have to anticipate some objection from physicians. Medical staff may object to reporting to this committee, in that the Medical Advisory Committee has the right to report *directly to the board*, through the Chief of Staff. However, people have seen that this right is not taken away by the Board's request that such reports be considered in detail first by its QA Committee.

The Board's committee is, according to the terms of reference, the meeting place for hospital and medical staff QA, QA and risk management (see Term 2), QA and Accreditation (4), and patient care and community or public relations (5). It has a significant role indeed, and leads one to insist that after the Management Committee, the QA Committee is the premier committee of the Board, before even the Finance Committee; because, of course, patient care is of more importance to a hospital Board than is finance! We can draw one further parallel with finance. The accreditation survey and report of CCHA is the QA Committee's equivalent of the annual auditor's report. It should be taken as a reflection of how well the Committee has been doing its job in demanding assurance of quality.

Although the Committee's terms of reference mention many individual responsibilities (accreditation, credentials, incidents and suits, for example), it has in reality but one essential role. The QA Committee is charged with the responsibility of examining, on behalf of the Board, the evidence of quality of care and service presented by the Chief of Staff and the CEO and *advising the Board on its appraisal* of what it has examined. If the Committee is assured as to their quality, it can probably carry the Board. If it is not, it is bound to tell those who reported to it, and advise the Board of its uncertainty or dissatisfaction.

3. Receiving Reports of the QA Program

3.1. QA as TA: Trustee Assurance

Findings of Quality Assurance activities throughout the facility shall be reported by the professional and other staff organizations to the governing body and management by a mechanism that does not conflict with normal executive reporting channels (*Standards*, p. 47, Reporting).

Although the board is the last link in the quality assurance chain, trustees derive almost as much benefit from QA and its reporting as do the hospital's practitioners. QA reports are intended "to ensure that the governing body fulfills its mandate in ensuring and being accountable for the delivery of optimal quality care" (*Standards*, p. 13).

In presenting QA to Boards of Trustees I have been able to dispense with any textbook definition of QA itself by saying that QA is whatever persuades or

The Hospital Board's QA Committee

The 1985 *Standards* for the Accreditation of Canadian Health Care Facilities state that "an institution-wide Quality Assurance Program is an essential element of Accreditation." They state further that the governing body shall be responsible for ensuring the carrying out of such a program.

So that it may be effective in discharging this responsibility, the Board should appoint a Quality Assurance Committee whose essential mandate would be that of monitoring the function of the institution's Quality Assurance activity and reporting to the Board on the process and the significant results of this monitoring. The suggested make-up of such a Committee would be:

(a) The Vice-chairman of the Board who shall chair the Committee;
(b) two additional lay trustees;
(c) the Chief of Staff or the Chief's delegate, from the Medical Advisory Committee (MAC);
(d) the Chief Executive Officer;
(e) the Director/Vice-president, Nursing.

As an alternative to the establishment of a separate committee, the Board may elect to expand the terms of reference of an existing committee to include Quality Assurance matters. Some committees already utilized for this purpose include: Management, Joint Conference, Patient Care, Accreditation or Public Relations Committees.

In either case, the following represent specific terms of reference for the Committee's Quality Assurance function.

It is recommended that the Quality Assurance Committee:

1. Receive and consider the monthly reports of the hospital's QA program and that of the MAC;

2. Receive and review all written complaints, serious incidents, suits and inquiries initiated against the hospital and its staff;

3. Report, at each regular meeting of the Board, current information about the quality of care and service being provided by the hospital and its medical staff;

4. Satisfy itself that the hospital is in compliance with appropriate legislation and is meeting the standards of the Canadian Council on Hospital Accreditation;

5. Prepare a report for the Annual Meeting of the Hospital Corporation concerning the scope and adequacy of the hospital's Quality Assurance Plan, and the quality of services being provided to the patients of the hospital.

gives them assurance about the quality of care and service provided by their facilities. "Quality assurance is trustee assurance." This fact implies several things about reporting QA to the board. Among these are:

3.1.1 Intelligibility. Most QA reports are generated by specialist departments. They need to be offered in the language of the intelligent generalist. This does not mean they have to be simple; they must be jargon-free.

3.1.2 Comprehensiveness.
The intent of QA is to demonstrate that all the bases are covered, that all significant services and programs are being reviewed on a continuing basis. Reporting should show the health of the whole enterprise, but should meet the test of significance.

3.1.3 Honesty.
U.S. authorities on QA recognize that in spite of all the hoopla of the QA program, it may be ineffective or, worse, a deception. Lois Bittle in comparing the "illusion of QA" with its reality noted

> paper compliance evidenced by little or no documented problem resolution, i.e.,
> - 1/3 of information to board non-essential
> - safe quality assurance reports
> - reluctance to report patient injury data
> - rubber stamp credentialling
> - no evidence of action taken (OHA, Toronto, May 18, 1986).

Another author used two terms

> to describe methods of avoiding or preventing perception of reality. They are *eyewash* and *white wash*. Eyewash is an attempt at making things look better than they are. Whitewash involves covering up unacceptable practices (Lamnin, 1983, p. 191).

While the honesty of QA reports is probably not so much a practical problem in Canada today as their comprehensiveness and intelligibility, it bears mention. QA is demanding that, for the first time, professionals sit on the same side of the table with lay trustees and tell them what they are doing and how well they are doing it. This frankness runs counter to decades of confidentiality and professional solidarity.

3.2. Four Elements in Quality Determination

Administrators and Chiefs of Staff in obedience to the demands of the Council are, in many hospitals, now making QA reports to the Board or its committee. Meanwhile the trustees are dutifully receiving these reports and are showing due appreciation. But in most places there is a root question that has neither been asked nor answered: what is it that convinces or assures the trustee? As soon as this question is asked the realization dawns that there is no single or overwhelming source of trustee assurance. As adults we make up our minds through an accumulation of evidence, on the basis of which a picture emerges. We cannot say what data trustees will receive, or which each will find most convincing, but we can point to certain classes of information that should be available to them and relevant to decisions about quality assurance.

There are the trustees' sense of the people doing the work, their understanding of the process and findings of the QA program, the implications of signal events and indicators, and persuasive opinions of qualified others. In the description of each below, these are labelled personal trust, the QA program, occurrence screening, and external assessment.

3.2.1 Personal Trust.
Trustee assurance or confidence is anchored on the elementary presumption that the professionals employed by the hospital are qualified and competent, are dedicated to the provision of high-quality patient care and institutional service, and are men and women of integrity, whose work and reports can be believed. The board will not assume that they are infallible because this would obviate the need for any QA program at all. Nor will it be surprised if from time to time professionals show a partiality or superior loyalty to their own profession or its members. These go with the territory. But the foundation of QA is personal trust.

If a QA program or trustee assurance were unable to start from this point, both would be continually undermined by uncertainty as to the integrity of the reports themselves: were they believable? Meanwhile, the QA program itself would be, for the professionals, an inquisitorial process that they would need to deceive or defeat. In QA, service providers, whose quality is being assessed and reported, and management, which is reviewing their achievements, belong on the same side of the table. In QA there is no *we* and *them*. Practitioners and management are both *we*, because all are taking responsibility and being held accountable for the care and service provided.

Obviously, trust in the professionals is not an invitation to gullibility. Trust originally given will be enhanced by evidence of performance, or it will be undermined by conflicting information from other sources. Trust is the place to start. But where is the dividing line between trust and gullibility? And, what can the board ask for as supporting evidence without questioning the professional integrity of, in particular, physicians?

Yesterday I had to go to the post office to pick up my latest Visa card. When I detached the plastic from its cover I noted the statement: "Your personal credit limit is $2,300; should you wish a higher credit limit . . . please contact your local branch." So $2,300 is the limit of my bank's personal trust in me at the present time. How it arrived at $2,300 I do not know, but I seem to remember that originally the limit was just a fraction of this sum. Presumably as the bank saw my habit of clearing my indebtedness promptly, it increased the limit again and again. If, however, my habits had run in the other direction, the bank may have held to the original limit until, by my spendthrift ways, I forced it to cancel my card altogether.

This is a good analogy for a hospital Board's trust in the professional. Trust is not a blank cheque, but the authorization to do good things; it is a business proposition. In the hospital environment, trust is repaid with evidence of good performance, and credit is replenished through intelligible, honest, and generally favourable reporting. Hospital Boards have not found it difficult to be businesslike in their dealings with their administrators. CEOs are clearly employees of the Board, and on a monthly basis render account of their administration, particularly of the hospital's finances. However, it has been much harder for trustees to exercise their trust prudently with physicians who are not employees and whose profession does not encourage prying eyes or the judgement of amateurs. Yet Boards have the duty to demand account of physicians, as they do administrators.

EXHIBIT 25

Roles and Competence in Medical Staff Review

	APPRAISING AGENCY	
SUBJECTS OF APPRAISAL	**MAC AND ITS COMMITTEES**	**BOARD OF TRUSTEES**
Individual Physicians	1. Clinical Practice	3. Personal Behaviour
Medical Groups Organized Departments	2. Medical Standards	4. Quality Assurance

Exhibit 25 expresses graphically the differing "Roles and Competence in Medical Staff Review." The figure suggests that the Board should depend on the MAC to pass judgement (1) on the *clinical practice* of individual physicians and (2) on the *medical*—or professional—*standards* set by and for various groups of physicians or organized departments. However, the board itself is competent (3) to judge the *personal behaviour* of individual practitioners and (4) the adequacy and usefulness of the *Quality Assurance* program or strategies in place in medical departments.

In the case of Squares 1 and 2, the trustees' questions to Chief of Staff, President or other officer are: How do you know? If occurrence X happened here, how would you know? How do these data convince you? What is the process you—your Committee—goes through to make this determination? Such questions say: "Show me/convince me." They are not evidence of prying or distrust, but they are requests to be taken into the confidence of the professional who has the duty of surveillance.

Squares 3 and 4 belong to the trustees. On occasion, Boards have to advise or decide on matters that touch on the individual rights of physicians, their interpersonal relations or personal behaviour. No professional qualifications are required to decide on matters of integrity, dignity or consideration, whether the physician is defendant or plaintiff.

Finally (4), trustees must soon become experts in *Quality Assurance*, in the review of programs and their processes and reports. Indeed, at Board level they own the program and have every right to say what they perceive and what improvements they can advise. Thus, trustees can find fault with the comprehensiveness of the program—for instance, in that neither Paediatrics nor Psychiatry was participating in the medical staff's audit program, or its *depth*—because audit activities in the Emergency department looked only at documentation, not the care itself. They can also review the remedial action proposed or completed, and ask for comparisons between surveillance systems practised by their MAC and those of comparable hospitals.

3.2.2 Quality Assurance Reports.

The second element in the trustee's confidence in the hospital's quality of care and service should be provided by its QA reports. Through the organized QA program, the medical staff and the clinical and support departments have the opportunity of demonstrating to the Board both the nature and quality of the care and service they are providing. This continuous process should, over time, give substance to the trust originally extended. The QA program should demonstrate the excellence of staff and the institution, the soundness of the care and services being given and, where possible, the character of the results. It should be possible for trustees to relate the material being presented to them with the central or principal functions of the hospital and its medical and other departments. In their review of these reports, trustees will be concerned about the three elements mentioned at the end of the last section: the comprehensiveness of the program, the depth or scope of the reviews and the adequacy of the remedial action.

3.2.3 Occurrence Screening.   If the first two elements in the trustees's picture of care are overwhelmingly positive and pro-hospital, elements #3 and #4 test them both. Occurrence Screening and External Assessments (next section) contradict or validate the hospital's and medical staff's claims and the confidence reposed in them both by the board.

Occurrence Screening is the title of a specific QA process originated in the U.S. whereby specially trained staff review current patient charts to identify "occurrences" or deviations from practice standards or expectations of patient outcome. These chart auditors expect or hope to identify the deviations early enough to present full-blown "events," in which harm is caused to patients or damage to the hospital and its resources. Few hospitals in Canada can afford to employ a team of staff to carry out this function, so that surveillance of "incidents" or occurrences has remained a function of the department, and screening of events has been assumed by QA.

U.S. authorities have defined an incident as

> any occurrence, accident or event, that is not consistent with normal patient care that either did or could directly result in an injury to a patient, employee, or visitor (Orlikoff, Fifer, and Greeley, 1981, p. 35).

Incidents or occurrences have three characteristics. They are (1) *observable*— a single event or series of events or occurrences; (2) *inconsistent* with normal patient progress, the provision of good care, and/or the maintenance of a safe, comfortable environment; (3) *injurious*, in that they injured or threatened to injure patients or visitors, hospital staff, and/or the physical, legal or financial integrity of the hospital.

News of some incidents or occurrences currently reach the Board through patient suits and complaints. Increasingly, however, under the auspices of both QA and Risk Management, hospital and medical departments will be expected to identify *zero standards* or events, i.e., results that should *never* occur—surgical complications, nosocomial infections, lost-time incidents, stock-outs, medication incidents, power failures, paycheque errors, equipment failures, lost specimens or reports, unsafe radiation, and so forth. Many of these are reported at the departmental level but are not part of QA reporting. Trustees need to know that zero standards have been established in all departments *and* that breaches of them will be reported monthly through the QA program.

3.2.4 External Assessments. There is little need to describe or explain this stratum of data again. We are referring here exclusively to two of the three categories of *quality approval* (Ch. IV, Sec. 4.3), to external reviews and patient/client responses. Although most external assessments are reviews of the hospital's processes and not its outcomes they tend to be reliable, independent, and highly credible to trustees. We recommended that all external assessments should be a part of every department's QA program, where possible. Their reports should be presented to the board/committee "unmassaged," i.e., in their original form with whatever translation the layman may require.

Figure 15 is intended to provide a graphic summary of the concurrence of information that mature QA programs should provide to their Boards. It suggests that trustee assurance is a determination based on the elements we have described above. Trustees will be looking primarily for a consistency in the stories reaching them from the various data sources. These will never spell perfection but a board may be assured if they demonstrate:

1. That the hospital/clinical staff are operating within expected norms for comparable facilities and services;

FIGURE 15

The Trustees' Four Degrees of Confidence

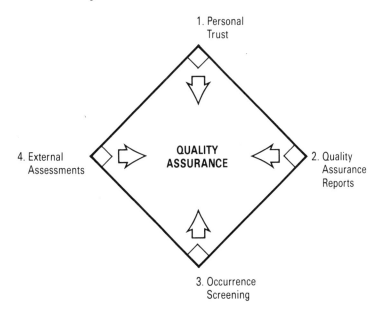

2. That clinical and administrative or support problems are being identified by the QA program;
3. That such problems are being successfully addressed; and
4. That there are a minimum of surprises.

3.3. Building the Picture

Assuming that there is a QA Committee of the board and it has its politics in hand, the next question is how or where it should start in order to make its own determination of the quality of the hospital's/medical staff's operation. At the risk of oversimplifying matters, I would recommend its making its determination based on the following (in descending order):

1. What external assessors say
2. What the hospital's leading indicators show
3. What the professionals say, and
4. What the clients say.

3.3.1 External Assessment.

There are three reasons for beginning with the demand to see or be informed about *all* external assessments. First, irrespective of any QA program, these data are readily available. Second, these assessments are authoritative, i.e., external agencies will act on the merits of what they perceive. And third, a board could be criticized for not knowing nor requiring action upon the most important of these assessments.

In order to build the picture the Committee may ask Administration to set up a calendar annually that will show what assessments are expected. Some assessments can only be plotted by year, such as the accreditation survey; some are entirely random, e.g., the narcotics inspection by Health and Welfare Canada. Thus, the layout of the calendar and its uses must be quite flexible. Its intent is to help the trustees to anticipate and manage these important data, and observe the blanks in the picture of external assessment.

3.3.2 Leading Indicators.

Secondly, the QA Committee should look for a quarterly report of leading indicators. These may be of two kinds: first, essential patient care statistics, and, second, occurrences or breaches of zero standards. These indicators will be developed in two ways. Zero standards can best be determined by medical staff committees (Exhibit 26) and hospital departments, who should be asked to identify these incidents or occurrences as part of the QA program and to report them through its reporting processes. Essential patient care statistics will come from the MAC and Administration and should be the statistics they review monthly to monitor the hospital's clinical performance. The Mississauga Hospital distributes a quarterly *Quality of Care Indicators Report* to its trustees. As the list of indicators (Exhibit 27) shows, the Report carries both essential patient care statistics (their "structure measures") and occurrences (their "outcome measures"). It also gives a summary of QA data recently reported (their "process measures").

EXHIBIT 26

Medical Staff Committees and Their Surveillance

COMMITTEE	OCCURRENCES* AND AUDIT TOPICS
1. Admission and Discharge (Utilization)	Long-stay cases* Cancellations and postponements* Emergency and very urgent admissions* Transfers to Extended Care facilities*
2. Continuing Care	Admission protocol Discharge and placement* Decubitus ulcers* Quality-of-life data
3. Emergency	Regular chart reviews Complaints* Delays in attention or consultation* Returns within twelve hours*
4. Infection Control	Post-operative wound infections* Urinary tract infections* Veneral disease* Bacterial enteric infections* TB* Infectious hepatitis* Other non-bacterial infections* Parasitic, fungal and other infections*
5. Medical Audit	Structured patient care appraisal studies Mini-audits, reviews of historical data
6. Medical Records	Content and quality of charting Guidelines for release of confidential information Overdue charts* Patient consents*
7. Operating Room	Post-operative pneumonia* Anaesthesia-related complications* Operative complications* Deaths* Transfers to other facilities* Post-operative wound infections*
8. Pharmacy and Therapeutics	New drugs and deletions to formulary Drug reactions* Medication incidents*
9. Tissue and Audit	Deaths* Unimproved cases* Transfers to other hospitals* Discrepancies between pre- and post-op Dx and tissue Dx* Cases with minimal pathology* Blood transfusion reactions* Operations on reproductive organs* Appendectomies* Complications* Errors in Dx*

*Occurrences or Incidents

EXHIBIT 27

The Quality of Care Indicators Report (from the Mississauga Hospital)

Table 1

Indicators presented in the Quality of Care Indicators Report

Structure measures
  Full-time staff turnover
  Average waiting time for admission
  Average monthly bed cancellation rate
  Average monthly postponements
  Average number of long-term patients in acute care beds
  Average number of patients in the Emergency Department at 0800 hours
    waiting for beds
  Percentage of acute care patients with a length-of-stay of 30 days or more

Process measures
  Medical care evaluation studies
  Concurrent nursing audits

Outcome measures
  Hospital-acquired general surgical infection rate
  Complication rate
  Adult death rate
  Post-operative death rate
  Newborn death rate
  Autopsy rate
  Medication incidents
  Patient incidents

Stacey, S., Henderson, M., and Markel, F. "Patient care indicators: involving trustees in QA." *Hospital Trustee* 9 (5) Sept.–Oct. 1985, pp. 24–26.

3.3.3 QA Reports.   In QA reports the professionals directly responsible for the care and service are, in effect, saying:

> In order to assess the quality of our care and service we assessed our performance in respect of (one significant aspect of a principal function). These are our results. . . . And this is what the results say to us. . . .

QA is first and foremost self-assurance based on assessment or audit. The professionals' sense of assurance is all-important because their sensitivity to the data will be more acute than that of anyone to whom the report is made. This does not remove the appropriateness of receivers of the report asking why professionals are satisfied with the standards they accept. Many of the common performance rates can be reviewed in the light of those accepted or obtained by nearby or peer hospitals/departments.

3.3.4 Client Data.   It is always appropriate for trustees to ask how patients and families perceive their care. These people will take back to their neighbours and friends stories of what the hospital was like. It is important that the Board knows what the community's perception is and acts in light of it. First, the QA Committee should have access to all written complaints and commendations received by Administration. Secondly, it should expect that all verbal complaints and commendations made to or brought to the attention of management will be documented immediately. As an elementary procedure of risk management, Administration should respond to all complaints and commendations within 24 hours and follow them up as necessary. Finally, the trustee's committee should, through the CEO, call on the hospital's QA Committee to develop an annual cycle in which patient opinions are sought of all the major services provided to them by the hospital, i.e., all aspects of patient care—medical care, nursing, radiology, emergency, physical medicine, laboratory and such services as food, admission, their accommodation and environment.

It is recommended that these program elements be put in place one by one, at the request of the trustees, so that they understand and master each, weighing their differing scope and validity. The trustees' or committee's intent is, on behalf of the full board, to examine all necessary data to determine and report to the board the quality of the hospital's performance.

4. Utilization Review

The contrast between hospitals in Canada and the U.S. is starkest at the level of utilization. In Canada, the problem is too much demand and too few resources. In the U.S., theirs is idle technology and empty beds. Whereas some big-city hospitals in Ontario operate for much of the year at over 100 percent capacity for medical-surgical beds, 60 percent occupancy is thought to be good for many acute facilities in the U.S. Because of this contrast, Utilization Review (UR) means something very different in the two countries. UR Coordinators are found in almost all U.S. hospitals. Their task is to review all services provided to patients, to ensure that there are no more than are necessary *and* reimbursible. Third-party payors (Blue Cross, company health plans, Medicare, etc.) employ UR Coordinators to review treatment services both prospectively and retrospectively. They are very sensitive to patients being over-doctored or over-serviced by hospitals.

The Canadian problem is no less severe, but it surfaces as high occupancy, lengthy delays in elective procedures, waiting lists for out-patient treatments, and, of course, deficit budgets. The Canadian Council on Hospital Accreditation rightly emphasizes Utilization Review and places primary responsibility for it with Medical Advisory Committees and their Admission and Discharge *or* Utilization subcommittees. Neither their expertise nor the importance given to the problem here match those encountered in the U.S.

5. Evaluating the Quality of Governance

This obligation is the sleeper in the battery of QA requirements in the 1985 *Standards*. It merits but two sentences in that publication and has tended to shrink into insignificance beside the mountain of activity within hospital departments and the difficulty of cajoling medical staff into more comprehensive QA endeavours. Yet there it is: the obligation of the Board to examine itself and its achievements. The demand that the hospital Board engage in self-appraisal is echoed by, or perhaps echoes, the sense of dissatisfaction with corporate boards, and, in the U.S., the rise of Nominating Committees whose mandate is to carry out regular evaluations of the Board.

Writing in *Hospital Trustee* (Wilson, 1985 [iii]), I identified four alternatives in Board evaluation. According to the literature, it is possible to appraise the Board as a whole *or* individual trustees, and both of them can appraise themselves *or* rely on others to carry out the appraisal. Most organizations and writers rely on self-appraisal, particularly when it concerns the Board as a whole. Significant exceptions to this are the Board Mentor program offered by provincial hospital associations in Canada, B.C., Alberta and Saskatchewan, and Ontario's Hospital Board Effectiveness Program (OHA, 1984). The leading models of both trustee and board self-appraisal come from the American Hospital Association (AHA, 1979; Moses, 1986) and the Maryland Hospital Education Institute (MHEI, 1977). The latter provided a rare example of appraisal of individual trustees, though it must be much more common formally (i.e., by Nominating Committees) than available sources would suggest.

CHAPTER IX

The Evaluation of the Hospital-wide Program

The youngest son of the family was bringing his girlfriend home for dinner. Jamie was eighteen, and his family had never even seen him out with a girl, although they knew he had dated quite a lot before this. As the family waited for him to arrive, there was a lot of speculation as to what Jamie's girlfriend was going to be like. In fact, they had been speculating about Elizabeth all week! His elder sisters all had views of what sort of girl Jamie would fall for— and he did seem to be very serious about her. Jamie's mother had her own views—or were they fears?—too. And all the while the father kept his peace. Then there was the sound of a key in the front door, and Jamie and Elizabeth came in. Speculation ceased. Yes, she was a brunette; no, she was pretty; yes, she was out-going, dressed well, quite small, and on and on.

By accident the Canadian Council on Hospital Accreditation made Canadian hospitals play the role of the family members to its Elizabeth (the QA program) for three years. Consider: at the Surveyors' Conference in March, 1983, the Council unveiled its new Quality Assurance Standards. In September, 1984, it revised them, but not until April, 1986, did it move beyond statements of principle to describe how to distinguish the real thing. Of course, the Council too was searching for reality along with hospitals in the program, and it showed what it knew in the fall of 1983 and winter of 1984 (CCHA, 1984). But Canadian QA is not just U.S. QA spoken more crisply, eh! It is a brand new program, and, as our health systems continue to diverge, likely to grow more distinct.

At the 1986 Surveyors' Conference, in Toronto, a Council staff member described the essential features surveyors should look for in the fully functioning QA program. She made four points:

First, QA programs at all levels need to be based on stated mission statements, goals and objectives, and quality standards.

Second, QA programs need to show good *documentation* of continuing *evaluation* of performance, on the basis of which *strengths* are demonstrated *and weaknesses* are followed up. News of this activity is *communicated* through the organization to the governing body.

Third, a QA program appropriate to a three-year award will have all the above elements in respect of:

- Governing body
- Administration
- Medical services
- Nursing services
- Environmental safety
- Emergency services
- Pharmacy departments

and *most* of the other departments and services.

Fourth, the Council handed out checklists covering structure evaluation and process and outcome evaluation. These lists indicated the appropriateness of each element to five classes of departments/services: Board and Administration, Medical, Nursing, Other Professionals, and Facility Support. The lists, without their application to these services, are reproduced in Exhibit 28.

Having completed the draft of this book and worked on implementing QA in about 15 hospitals, the author was intensely interested in the Council's presentation. Was it time to go back to the drawing board? More important, were hospitals employing the adult learning model going to have to change

---

EXHIBIT 28

Elements Expected in a QA Program

EVALUATION (STRUCTURE)	1. Policy Procedure/By-law	6. Environment Safety
	2. Performance Appraisal	7. Preventive Maintenance
	3. Credentialling	8. Transfer Function
	4. Delineation/Renewal of Privileges	9. Effectiveness of Meetings
	5. Continuing Education	
EVALUATION (PROCESS/ OUTCOME)	1. Criteria Audits	6. Medical Records Control
	2. Occurrent Screening	7. Death Review
	3. Incident Reporting	8. Tissue Review
	4. Infection Control	9. Utilization Review, etc.
	5. Drug Control	

their programs to bring them into line with the recommendations of the Council? While CCHA's terminology and that used in this book differ in places, only two differences in strategy are apparent. The adult learning model is constructed on the basis of Principal Functions rather than Goals and Objectives, as stipulated by the Council. Secondly, standards for us are set with reference to actual audits or quality control procedures. They are not free-standing as could be inferred from their place in the Council's picture.

In the main, however, the QA model described in this book looks remarkably like what CCHA would have surveyors look for. In addition, news from hospitals recently surveyed support the perception of there being a close fit. Surveyors have expressed considerable satisfaction with what they have found in ALM hospitals. As to Principal Functions versus Goals and Objectives and *ad hoc* Standards versus the pre-packaged variety, I have advised our hospitals to maintain what is *working well* for them and justify their choices to the surveyors.

What was most satisfying about the Council's QA outline was in the fundamental choice it signified. There was always the danger that the Council could have opted for a high documentation model, and defined the acceptable program in terms of its manuals, written plans, and quantities of standards and reports. Instead it chose a dynamic model, high on purposeful assessment and remediation, insistent on closing the loop by effective reporting to board level, and strong on the integration of elements in place. It is largely the philosophical concurrence of the Council's model with ours that suggested little need for sudden revision.

This final chapter outlines how the author would evaluate a QA program and provides a useful recapitulation of many of the issues and recommendations made in earlier chapters.

1. QA and the Board

1.1. *A report is made to the Board at each of its regular meetings indicating the quality assurance status of the hospital.*

1.2. *The report is presented by the Board committee charged with responsibility for reviewing quality assurance reports from the hospital and the medical staff.*
   The first essential of a functioning QA program is that regular reports are being rendered to the hospital's Board of Trustees. We will have more to say about the character of the reports, the response of the Board and the meaning of regularity—the point to be made here is that there is no functioning system in place until QA is reported to the Board. There will be all sorts of useful components, but no system, no hospital-wide QA program. Thus, in evaluating the hospital's QA program, the first place to look is in the official minutes of the Board.
   At Board level, I would like to find evidence that QA was reported at each regular meeting by a trustee member of the committee of the Board charged

with the responsibility of reviewing hospital and medical data monthly. If QA is reported directly to the Board there will, by force of circumstances, be less data reported and less serious consideration given to them. An examiner will, of course, be very interested to see how the Board responds to reports on QA. Does it merely receive the reports and make appreciative noises, or has it developed a maturity in handling these data, that allows it to respond appropriately to them and so complete the loop by sending messages back to those who originated the item? This is the goal.

2. The Board's QA Committee

2.1. *The Board committee receives reports about all organized departments of the hospital, according to a schedule drawn up by the CEO, and all committees of the MAC and departments of the medical staff, according to a schedule submitted by the Chief of Staff.*

2.2. *The Board committee receives news of the status of departmental QA programs and of the assessments carried out to monitor the quality of their performance.*

2.3. *The Board committee reviews all incidents, inquiries and suits that are reportable to the Board, all reports of inspections/appraisals of the hospital and its departments carried out by outside agencies, especially the periodic survey reports of the Canadian Council on Hospital Accreditation.*

2.4. *The Board committee presents a report to the Annual General Meeting of the hospital corporation on the quality of patient care provided in and by the hospital, the hospital's accreditation status, and the scope and effectiveness of the hospital's QA program.*

It will be necessary to go to the minute book of the QA Committee, whatever its name, for answers to these more detailed questions. At this level, the examiner should be looking at the character of the reports reaching the trustees, before they are summarized by the QA Committee. He or she will want to see evidence that three types of information are being reviewed with this committee:

1. Reports on the hospital's *performance* in providing care or service. These will usually review the measurement of some aspects of a specific program or department function, against predetermined criteria.
2. Progress reports on the development of the hospital's QA *program*. The accent should be on the attainment of successive levels of compliance with a model of program development.
3. An analysis of hospital *incidents* (complaints, suits, occurrences) that are reportable to the Board. Although more embarrassing incidents may be considered initially by the management committee, it is appropriate that the QA Committee reviews them also. Incidents usually say something

about the quality of the hospital's performance which is the Committee's concern, and the QA Committee focusses on remedies and improvement and not liability, which is a further justification for it to review all incidents.

Although it is not easy to find, examiners will be interested in evidence that the QA Committee is in control of its affairs and not responsive alone to the professionals who report to it. Is the committee being snowed by detailed and sophisticated data, or is it receiving reports that present findings and implications in layman's terms, so that trustees can participate fully in the discussion?

3. The Medical Advisory Committee (MAC)

3.1. *The MAC has a current QA plan for the medical staff which includes,* inter alia, *a schedule according to which it will receive reports on quality assurance issues from organized departments and MAC subcommittees.*

3.2. *Organized departments of the medical staff undertake medical/surgical audits and other evaluative studies according to a protocol drawn up by the Medical Audit and Tissue Committee.*

3.3. *MAC Committees establish standards, criteria and quality indicators within the mandate indicated by their terms of reference, and report the results of their monitoring of such standards as frequently as determined by the MAC.*

True story: one time I needed to check on a board's procedure with respect to the reappointment of members of the hospital's medical staff. Yes, they did do it annually, early in the calendar year. Yes, there was a motion to that effect on the books for the current year. Was there a list, I wondered, of those reappointed? Well, it wasn't attached to the board minutes. No problem, I thought, it will be attached to the Chief of Staff's Report. No, it wasn't there, in part because the Chief of Staff never made a formal report; he simply made an oral presentation of the highlights of the MAC minutes. Well, it will be attached to them, of course? Actually, no. The MAC had just endorsed a recommendation received from the Credentials Committee. The minutes of this last committee were not available. They were kept in the Chief's office. I just hoped to heavens there was a list of the *sixty* doctors somewhere. Bad story.

In evaluating medical staff QA, surveyors have a right to see a Chief's report that is distinct from the MAC minutes. Personally, I would like to see both the Chief's report *and* subcommittee reports (such as Audit and Tissue, P&T, etc.) to the MAC divided into (1) QA and (2) management issues. The order does not matter, but there does need to be a distinction between QA implications and day-to-day operating problems.

So much for reporting; how about the substance of the QA program? We should look for three things: structure, depth and scope. If a MAC is serious about QA, it will have a schedule that indicates by month when it expects reports (1) of clinical audits and (2) of its principal subcommittees. It should be possible to validate this schedule by reference to recent MAC minutes.

The Medical Audit and Tissue (MAT) Committee is often left in sole charge of medical staff QA, and is expected to interpret or report all audits to the MAC. Some MATs act in a different capacity, that of an audit facilitator, to see organized departments (medicine, surgery, etc.) report their own audits directly to the MAC. In this scheme of things, MAT would set the schedule of audits in consultation with the departments, and assist them to carry them out and to learn and improve in the audit process by experience. People are always interested in numbers—how many audits a medical staff should complete in a year. If a staff is large enough to do a meaningful audit, i.e., it has at least 12 members on its active staff, then it should do four per annum (one per quarter). If the staff is departmentalized, then it could aim for two audits per department and three or four from General Practice, per year. This is the sort of depth I would expect in a mature medical staff QA program.

The scope of medical staff QA is represented by the committees whose concerns cut across departments: Admission and Discharge, Utilization, Medical Records, Pharmacy and Therapeutics, Credentials, Infection Control, Emergency, etc. It is important that these committees recognize that they have a role in monitoring *quality* as well as operations, and identify topics for audits they will sponsor or will recommend to appropriate departments. When these committees develop a quality focus, they provide a horizontal dimension to medical staff QA, which compliments the vertical organization by department. This is more than a matter of geometry. Many hospitals have seen medical audit flare and burn with great enthusiasm for a year, only to smoulder and die the next. Lack of topics, lack of board support, lack of follow-through are given as the causes.

MAC committees can provide this kind of support and keep alive what would otherwise be single departmental audits. As indicated (Section 3.3 above) these committees should be reporting specific indicators, of their choice to the MAC on a scheduled basis, and with these data point up quality issues as they occur.

4. The Hospital's QA Committee

4.1. *The QA Committee reports monthly to the CEO on the status and development of the hospital's QA program and the performance of clinical and support departments as demonstrated by structured assessments.*

4.2. *The QA Committee receives reports from hospital departments according to a schedule agreed with them annually.*

4.3. *The QA Committee receives reports from hospital-wide programs, such as occupational health and safety.*

4.4. *The QA Committee is expected to encourage departments to follow up on negative or unsatisfactory findings on their own and in the audit of others, so that problems can be solved prior to their reporting to the CEO.*

When I think about hospital QA Committees, my immediate response is *paper*, filing cabinets full, bookshelves full of QA binders, full of QA papers. The surveyors or QA program evaluators have a real role here. They need to talk the dynamics of the program and not its systems. How is it organized, what does it report, what results can it point to in the delivery of care or service? We need to talk people, not paper. But equally, if we denigrate the paper they are proud of, we have rejected them as people. We need to see both and help QA leaders to value the dynamic, as opposed to the historical, elements in quality assurance.

We should expect to find a QA Committee composed largely of department heads, which manages the QA program and provides the link between departmental quality assurance and the CEO. It sets a schedule under which departments will report their QA activity, according to differing frequencies. It evaluates the quality of their submissions before forwarding them to the CEO *en route* to the board. Examiners will look for evidence of this sort of structure in terms of reference, reporting schedules, and committee minutes.

Next, they will look at the substance of the department's report. Is there evidence that departments are engaged in the regular *assessment* of performance in their principal functions? Are there examples of their carrying out topic-focussed *audits*, in the interests of problem solving or program evaluation? How expert and appropriate are their methods of measuring performance? How involved are general staff in the carrying out of audits or assessments? Most of these questions should be answered from the departmental reports held by the QA Committee.

It is worth questioning the integration of nursing with hospital QA. Because CCHA demanded audits in nursing many years (1977) before it did of the rest of hospital departments, nursing has had a head start, but also has been pointed in a different direction to that outlined in the 1985 *Standards*. The problems this has created for nursing have been discussed in Chapter V. Our first concern here is to see that, rather than have two unrelated programs—Nursing Audits *versus* other department QA—both sectors should be talking the same language and doing the same things, even though with differing emphasis. Second, it is essential that the findings are discussable between nursing and other clinical and support departments, so that problems of cooperation are reviewed, and hopefully some multidisciplinary audits undertaken.

Finally, we must ask the question: at what QA level are hospital departments operating? In earlier chapters, we outlined six levels or stages, from start-up to the fully developed program. Optimally, a hospital should have all programs or departments operating at least at or close to the fifth level. This would mean that all were generating reportable performance data on a monthly basis, and were reporting in line with a schedule determined by the QA Committee. Further, these departments should be using a variety of assessment methods, among which criteria-based measurements predominate.

5. Hospital Departments

5.1. *Each department is responsible to Administration for developing a QA plan under which it will set standards, promote quality of performance, monitor activity and assess its achievements in respect of its principal functions.*

5.2. *Departments report their quality assurance activities regularly to Administration. These reports are considered by the QA Committee.*

5.3. *Departments seek to employ all members of their staff in their QA programs, as committee members, assessors, quality monitors and on panels developing standards for performance.*

5.4. *Departments appraise the achievements of their QA programs annually, so as to increase their effectiveness and ensure that they are appropriate to the principal functions of the department.*

The hallmarks of a good departmental QA program are planning, participation, the use of a variety of methods to achieve and monitor quality, and a demonstrable return on investment. In Chapter IV we described the four essential components of quality assurance and in Chapter V used the same components in the development of the department's QA plan. It makes sense therefore to complete the loop, and look at the department's implementation—how it has set standards and goals, promoted their acceptance, monitored its principal functions and assessed the department's performance.

Throughout this text, stress has been laid on the central role of general staff and line professionals as those who practise quality. Quality assessment should register the extent to which they achieve the standards set for them, but we also need to know the extent to which they participated in standard setting and performance evaluation. If the department has its own QA committee, are general staff prominently represented?

In looking at performance monitoring and assessing, an appraiser may want to see some variety in the methods used for quality measurement, but that should be related to the functions being assessed rather than out of a desire for novelty.

By "return on investment" we mean simply, "Was the endeavour worthwhile? If so, how valuable?" Clearly, you can have a good QA program that does not return much in either problems or remedies, but not for long. If staff and management have derived little benefit in problems solved and questions answered, it will not be long before motivation begins to lag and participation fall off. Whether program evaluation is self-evaluation or done by an outsider, serious attention should be paid to its success in discovering practical truths and solving operating problems.

6. The Hospital's QA Plan

Most QA authorities are more concerned than is the writer about the shape and availability of the hospital's written QA Plan required by CCHA in the 1983 and 1985 *Standards*. It is time to repair this deficiency in the account to date.

From the author's perspective, the hospital's QA Plan is not one piece of cloth, but a patchwork quilt. The shape of the entire quilt is known ahead of time, and the general shape and number of the individual pieces, but their colours and textures depend on whose sewing box they came from. Though it sounds strange, the Program precedes the Plan in my model. The Plan legitimizes what has occurred and has been found to work. The Plan describes the Program to the outsider, as a map will point out the sights to the tourist. Thus we start with the Program and work with it, so that it encourages, monitors and tests the quality of performance, and reports results and asks advice and pursues problems until they are solved. All well and good, but what notes are written in the margin; what explanation is left of all this activity?

In a looseleaf binder in the Administrator's office should be found:

1. A statement issued by the Board endorsing the principle of Quality Assurance.
2. The terms of reference of the QA Committee of the Board—whatever its name.
3. An organizational chart detailing the method by which accountability for quality will be referred throughout the hospital and its medical staff to the Board.
4. Annual reports of the Board committee presented to annual general meetings of the hospital corporation.
5. Statements, policies, procedures and reporting schedules that detail the organization of QA for the medical staff.
6. The terms of reference of the hospital's QA Committee, its membership, and QA policy statements drafted by the Committee and signed by the Administrator.
7. The QA Committee's current 12-month plan which details the Committee's expectations of departmental QA programs and the current level of their compliance.
8. Filed in the order of the accreditation standards (essential elements, diagnostic and therapeutic elements, support elements and special case services), the QA Plan developed by each department and endorsed by the QA Committee. Although these plans will be broadly similar, I would be disappointed if they just sat there, as if they had all come out of the same mould!

Provided the linkages are strong and flexible, the individual programs can be changed as practice dictates.

7. Marks of Second-generation QA

At QA conferences and our institutes at OHA in 1986, the questions that were still being asked insistently come from the infancy or childhood of QA rather than from its adolescence or adulthood. But infancy and childhood pass quickly; what will adolescence show us? There are six developments which will probably distinguish a more mature program.

First, at departmental level, we can expect to see all programs operating at level six, that is working off a fully articulated QA Plan that is based on principal functions and relates all the standard documentation (job descriptions, policy and procedure manuals, etc.) to the promotion and maintenance of quality of performance. These QA Plans will mesh with the hospital's QA Plan, because annually, departmental plans will be discussed with and approved by the hospital QA Committee.

Second, at QA Committee level, we will see two changes. The first will be in membership. Many of the original members will have rotated off the Committee. After their hard job of getting the motor running, they will have earned their reward! Coincidentally, the focus of the Committee will have shifted from energizing and coaching, to evaluating and teaching. Start-up and compliance are issues of the past; now the concern is for the quality of quality assessment. This means more appropriate evaluation, more attention to outcome questions and assessment features built into the routines of work and the design of projects.

Third, we can look for some developments to occur *between* hospital and medical QA. While the division may make sense professionally and organizationally, it has never made sense clinically. We should look for an important series of multidisciplinary audits to occur under the sponsorship of either the MAC or the QA Committee. They may eventually take on a life and organization of their own under joint sponsorship and the coordination of Medical Records. While this development will be most successful if it seems to occur naturally, by accident, as it were, it is a development to be nurtured in the interests of all and especially the patient.

Fourth, QA reporting will become more efficient. In the last chapter we mentioned the quarterly reporting system developed by the Mississauga Hospital for its board. In a convenient shorthand that hospital has put together leading indicators, standard operating data and information generated by QA processes. I expect that many hospitals will already be doing much the same and that the reporting model adopted will match the complexity of the hospital's clinical role.

Fifth, there will be a pronounced tilt towards Risk Management (RM). Today insurers of hospitals want them to have programs in place that will lower the volume and severity of occurrences, assist in the management of claims and provide a good defence posture. Insurers may not know what QA is, may not be impressed with its relevance to their need, but want Risk Management strategies *now*. QA professionals have an obligation to demonstrate the applicability of QA strategies to the goals of RM. It is not that one is a subset of the other, so much as their sharing such common elements as occurrence screening, incident reporting, problem resolution, continuous assessment of principal functions, environmental safety, etc. If RM demands make QA less research-oriented and more hard-nosed and practical, that is acceptable. But we will all have lost if RM programs were to develop a complete life of their own, as they enjoy in the U.S., unrelated to hospital-wide quality assurance.

Finally, one day boards will formally evaluate the hospital's QA program, and make an annual report to the hospital corporation and the public on the quality of care provided in and by the hospital. When this occurs, as many times we have insisted that it should, the wheel will have gone full circle and the dreams of the authors of the 1983 *Standards* will be reality.

References

American Hospital Association. *Hospital Board Development Program*, Vol. 2, Unit 2: Assessing the performance of the board and its members. Chicago: AMA, 1977 and 1981.

Canadian Council on Hospital Accreditation. *Guide to Hospital Accreditation 1977* (Ottawa: CCHA, 1977).

Canadian Council on Hospital Accreditation. *Standards for Accreditation of Canadian Health Care Facilities, January 1983* (Ottawa: CCHA, 1983).

Canadian Council on Hospital Accreditation. *Proceedings of the Seminars on Quality Assurance* (Ottawa: CCHA, 1984a).

Canadian Council on Hospital Accreditation. *Standards for Accreditation of Canadian Health Care Facilities, 1985* (Ottawa: CCHA, 1984).

Crosby, P. *Quality is Free: The art of making quality certain* (New York: New American Library, 1979).

Crosby, P. *Quality without Tears: The art of hassle-free management* (New York: McGraw-Hill, 1984).

Donabedian, A. *The Definition of Quality and Approaches to Its Assessment.* Explorations in quality assessment and monitoring, Volume I (Ann Arbor, MI: Health Administration Press, 1980).

Guaspari, J. *I Know It When I See It: A modern fable about quality* (New York: AMACOM, 1985).

Lakein, A. *How to Get Control of Your Time and Your Life* (New York: Signet, 1974).

Lamnin, M. *Quality Assurance in Hospital Pharmacy: Strategies and techniques* (Rockville, MD: Aspen, 1983).

Maryland Hospital Education Institute. *Steps to Self-evaluation of Hospital Board Performance.* Lutherville, MD: MHEI, 1977.

Moses, R.P. *Evaluation of the Hospital Board and the Chief Executive Officer.* Chicago: American Hospital Publishing, 1986.

National Health and Welfare. *Dietetic Department Guidelines in Smaller Health Care Facilities* (Ottawa: National Health and Welfare, 1979).

National Health and Welfare. *Canada's Food Guide: Handbook (Revised)* (Ottawa: National Health and Welfare, 1982).

Ontario Hospital Association. *The Health-care Housekeeper* (newsletter of the Ontario Health-care Housekeepers' Association) 15 (1), January, 1985.

Ontario Hospital Association. "The Hospital Board Effectiveness Program." Slide-tape (15 min), 1984.

Ontario Hospital Association. *Quality Assurance and the 1983 Standards* (Toronto: OHA, 1984).

Ontario Hospital Association. *Quality Assurance: Getting Started* (Toronto: OHA, 1985).

Ontario Hospital Association and Ontario Dietetic Association. *Nutrition and Food Service Quality Assurance: Getting Started* (Toronto: OHA, 1986).

Orlikoff, J.E., Fifer, W.R. and Greeley, H.P. *Malpractice Prevention and Liability Control for Hospitals.* Chicago: American Hospital Association, 1981.

Stacey, S., Henderson, M., and Markel, F. "Patient care indicators: Involving trustees in QA." *Hospital Trustee* 9 (5), Sept.–Oct. 1985, pp. 24–26.

Warden, Gail. "Board self-assessment: Changing the governing structure to meet changing times." *Hospital Trustee,* March 1978, pp. 37–40.

Wilson, C.R.M. "Looking in the mirror: Evaluating boards and trustees." *Hospital Trustee* 9 (6) Nov.–Dec. 1985, 7–8.

Bibliographies

Such is the volume of writing on QA that bibliographies retain their currency for a relatively short time—a year or so. Accordingly, I have chosen not to give a list of the references that informed my discovery of QA in 1984 and 1985. Instead, students and practitioners of QA are directed to three sources which will maintain up-to-date bibliographies or indexes. They are:

1. The Canadian Association of Quality Assurance Professionals (CAQAP). Address: Suite 480, 151 Bloor Street West, Toronto, Ontario M5S 1T3.

The CAQAP issued its *Periodical Index for Quality Assurance in Canadian Health Care* in September, 1986, and stated its intention to update the *Index* annually. Its first edition (1986) carries over 600 references arranged by department and specialty (55 sections), and one general section on QA Management.

2. The National Association of Quality Assurance Professionals (NAQAP). Address: 1800 Pickwick Avenue, Glenview, IL 60025, U.S.A.

The NAQAP published its study guide, *Quality Assurance, Utilization and Risk Management,* in 1986 for those who wish to sit the certification examination for the professional designation: CPQA (Certified Professional in Quality Assurance). The Study Guide includes a seven-page general bibliography whose value lies in its intent to list basic or essential titles. Its focus is essentially the U.S. health care system with DRGs (Diagnosis Related Groups) and Prospective Payment, and the Standards of the Joint Commission, but the Canadian reader should have little problem selecting the more applicable references.

3. The Joint Commission on the Accreditation of Hospitals (JCAH). Address: 875 North Michigan Avenue, Chicago, IL 60611, U.S.A.

The JCAH publishes monthly the *Quality Review Bulletin* (QRB) which carries articles of differing subjects and complexity. Canadian readers are directed to its December issue each year, which contains the subject and author index for that year. The QRB publishes ten-year cumulative indexes also.

Articles by Christopher Wilson on Quality Assurance Topics

1984   (i) "Roles for an effective board: A five-finger exercise." *Hospital Trustee* 8 (1 & 2), Jan.–Feb., Mar.–Apr. 1984.

      (ii) "The purpose and structure of hospital-wide quality assurance." Paper No. 2 in *Quality assurance and the 1983 Standards* (Toronto: OHA, 1984), 7–25.

1985   (i) "Ninety days to a functioning QA program." *Health Care* 27(4), May 1985, 31–35.

      (ii) *Quality Assurance: Getting Started* (Toronto: OHA, 1985).

      (iii) "Making organizational changes 'user-friendly'." *Health Management Forum* 6(3), Autumn, 1985, 32–38 (topic: the Adult Learning Model)

      (iv) "Looking in the mirror: Evaluating boards and trustees." *Hospital Trustee* 9(6) Nov.–Dec. 1985, 7–8.

1986   "The role of the board of directors/trustees in the quality assurance program." *Australian Clinical Review* 21 (6), June 1986, 62–68.

1987   "Assessing quality in the 'Soft Services'." *Dimensions in Health Service 64* (4), May 1987, 38–39.

      "Evaluating QA reports: Five standards." (Under review.)

Index